Lighthouses

OF THE

Mid-Atlantic Coast

Your Guide to the Lighthouses of
New York, New Jersey, Maryland,
Delaware, and Virginia

Text by Elinor DeWire
Photography by Paul Eric Johnson

A Pictorial
Discovery Guide

Voyageur Press

Text © 2002 by Elinor DeWire
Photography © 2002 by Paul Eric Johnson, unless otherwise noted

Edited by Amy Rost-Holtz
Designed by Andrea Rud
Printed in China

02   03   04   05   06   5   4   3   2   1

Library of Congress Cataloging-in-Publication Data
DeWire, Elinor, 1953–
    Lighthouses of the Mid-Atlantic coast : your guide to the lighthouses of New York, New Jersey, Maryland, Delaware, and Virginia / text by Elinor DeWire ; photography by Paul Eric Johnson.
        p. cm. — (Pictorial discovery guide)
Includes bibliographical references and index.
    ISBN 0-89658-570-0 (hardcover)
    1. Lighthouses—Middle Atlantic States—Pictorial works.
I. Title. II. Series.
    VK1024.M54 D48 2002
    387.1'55'0975—dc21

                              2002002626

Distributed in Canada by Raincoast Books
9050 Shaughnessy Street, Vancouver, B.C. V6P 6E5

Published by Voyageur Press, Inc.
123 North Second Street, P.O. Box 338
Stillwater, MN 55082 U.S.A.
651-430-2210, fax 651-430-2211
books@voyageurpress.com
www.voyageurpress.com

Educators, fundraisers, premium and gift buyers, publicists, and marketing managers: Looking for creative products and new sales ideas? Voyageur Press books are available at special discounts when purchased in quantities, and special editions can be created to your specifications. For details contact the marketing department at 800-888-9653.

Frontispiece: Towering over its antique fogbell, comely Cove Point Lighthouse still stands watch on the Chesapeake Bay at Lusby, Maryland.

Title page: The cottage-style East Point Lighthouse at Heislerville, New Jersey, keeps vigil at the confluence of the Maurice River and the Delaware Bay.

Title page, inset: A nineteenth-century work of art in glass, the fourth-order Fresnel lens of Drum Point Lighthouse today sheds light on a bygone era as a museum piece on the grounds of Calvert Marine Museum. The red sector, created by the panel behind the lens, once marked dangerous shoals in the Chesapeake Bay near Solomons, Maryland.

Opposite the contents page: Hooper Strait Lighthouse reposes under a full moon.

Contents page, inset: Silhouetted at sunset, the 1885 Delaware Breakwater East Lighthouse gave up its duties in 1996. Like many old lighthouses, technology has rendered it obsolete.

Dedications

To Jonathan, Jessica, and Scott—the brightest lights in my life —ED

To Edna Charlotte Johnson —PEJ

Acknowledgments

The author wishes to thank the following individuals and organizations for their kind assistance in the preparation of this book: Tom Laverty and Yvonne Miller of the New Jersey Lighthouse Society; Robert Muller of the Long Island Chapter of the U.S. Lighthouse Society; Anne Puppa of the Chesapeake Chapter of the U.S. Lighthouse Society; Wayne Wheeler of the U.S. Lighthouse Society; Bob Trapani of the Delaware Bay & River Lighthouse Foundation; Carole Reily of the Delaware Bay Lighthouse Keepers & Friends Association; Tim Harrison of the American Lighthouse Foundation; Douglass Alves of the Calvert Marine Museum; Steve Murray and Betty Mugnier of the Hereford Inlet Lighthouse; Tom Hoffman of the National Park Service; Tricia Wood of Montauk Point Lighthouse; Dr. Robert Brown and the staff of the U.S. Coast Guard Archives; Cindy Herrick and the staff of the U.S. Coast Guard Academy Library; Paul O'Pecko and the staff of the Blunt White Library; the staff of the National Lighthouse Center and Museum; the staff of the Mariners Museum; Angelo Rigazio; Sally Snowman; Jim Crowley; Kim Ruth; the late Jim Gowdy; and Ken Black. A special thank you goes to Amy Rost-Holtz for her patience, good sense of humor, and hard work during the editing process, and to Paul Johnson for his fine insights and images of lighthouses throughout the Mid-Atlantic. As always, I am grateful to my family—Jonathan, Jessica, Scott, Kristin, and Rebecca—for their interest in and support of my work. —ED

Thank you to Chief Dennis Dever and the Aids to Navigation Team at Cape May for the pleasure in joining their endeavors for a day; Bob Trapani of the Delaware Bay & River Lighthouse Foundation for his help in understanding the operation, maintenance, and preservation of bay lights; Tom Hoffman of the National Park Service for enthusiastically providing some historical perspective; Douglass Alves of the Calvert Marine Museum, Thomas Ambrosio of the Montauk Historical Society, and Pete Lesher of the Chesapeake Bay Maritime Museum for sharing their resources; Betty Mugnier and Steve Murray's friendly welcome to Hereford Inlet Lighthouse; Robert Muller of the Long Island Chapter of the U.S. Lighthouse Society and Anne Puppa of the Chesapeake Chapter for the depth of their knowledge of the lighthouses and where to find them; Captain Buddy Norris for his perfectly timed tour of Chesapeake Bay; Carole Reily for the invitation to attend the Delaware Bay Lighthouse Keepers' outings; Lightkeeper Mike Oliviere at Hudson-Athens Lighthouse; Ed Weber of the Save the Esopus Meadows Lighthouse Commission; Gregory Bell of the Hudson River Maritime Museum; John Starling at Old Cape Henry Lighthouse; and Alice and Myles Hillary at Tinicum Rear Range Light. Thanks also to Amy Rost-Holtz for her sensitive eyes and help in keeping all the waters smooth, and to Elinor DeWire, especially for her sense of the qualities of lighthouses. —PEJ

Photographic Notes

When photographing, I like to keep it simple and respond as directly as possible to instinct and the environment. I used a 35-mm camera with a few lenses, occasional light reflectors or flashes, an often-too-heavy tripod, and Fuji's Velvia and Provia slide films. Keeping it spontaneous, I traveled about freely, taking only what shots were available at the time, and returning with the changing weather and seasons.

Early September is usually serene and often clear with beautiful skies. As I worked through the first week of the month, I felt at ease, with just enough creative tension to enhance expression. Then one morning there was an odd stillness to the air on Chesapeake Bay. In the bright light, a Navy cruiser appeared in the camera frame. Between the keeper's house and light tower it lingered. Later in the day I heard about the attacks on New York and Washington D.C. Cove Point with its Coast Guard radio station was locked down, and I headed home.

The task of shooting lighthouse photos became doubly challenging with the sudden uncertainty created by the September 11 events. Many of the lighthouses shared locales with now-sensitive facilities (such as nuclear plants and military bases), and people upon whom my plans depended had new priorities. Opportunities were rescheduled, and some sites were now closed to me. I received a phone call from the FBI's new inter-agency task force saying they had had reports of "a man with a telescope," and I needed to assure them I actually was just a lighthouse photographer with a camera and telephoto lens. American flags flying everywhere were company for my trips.

In the light of recent world events, lighthouses may seem trivial to some. For others, including me, America's lighthouses—and the hope they symbolize—have become even more significant. The world has definitely changed. But when surrounded by marsh grasses as far as I can see, with the ocean lapping at my feet, and a distant beacon alight against the sun's fading colors, I can imagine the way it was before. —Paul Eric Johnson

A light morning fog softly veils Hudson River and Roundout Lighthouse. Its flag ripples gently at half-mast in the autumn breeze—a tribute to the many lives lost on September 11, 2001.

Contents

Seeking a Safe Harbor

The night is dark, and I am far from home.
John Henry Newman (1801–1890), "Lead Kindly Light"

The bow of the fifty-foot motor launch bumped gently against the lighthouse dock, bobbing like a cork in the green-brown slurry stirred up by the rip of incoming tide. Opalescent moon jellies pulsed against the rocks, unfazed by the clamorous churn of diesel engines and the shouts of the crew. Angelo Rigazio, camera bag in hand, leaped onto the new fiberglass deck and uttered a soft whistle of surprise. Above him, the eighty-five-foot Harbor of Refuge Lighthouse pierced the blue sky. A tiered hulk of concrete, metal, and glass, the Delaware Bay lighthouse was his home from 1972 to 1973.

As the light's last officer in charge, Rigazio had made a final entry in the station logbook in December 1973, taken down the flag, locked the door, and given the venerable old sentry a final salute. He never expected to come back, especially as an honored guest, a celebrity of sorts with the Delaware River & Bay Lighthouse Foundation.

Bob Trapani, the foundation's president, offered a set of keys.

"Thought you might like to do the honors."

Rigazio's broad smile betrayed his delight. On this day, June 25, 2001, Harbor of Refuge Lighthouse wore a fresh coat of paint, as if dressed up to meet its old friend. It sported a new gallery railing and solar panels to power the beacon, and it could look forward to a more intensive facelift in the coming months. The new dock and stairway had been completed, and plans were in place to restore the interior.

Since his departure nearly thirty years before, Rigazio watched the beacon night after night from his home in Cape May, seventeen miles east. In the decades since automation, the lighthouse had become ramshackle, an eyesore. Paint peeled, rust stains rippled down the walls, windows were boarded up. The caisson was battered on the seaward side where a ship hit it in 1986, and the dock had become a mangle of corroded metal and broken concrete.

"It was always different for land lights," Rigazio mused. "People could get to them easier, I guess, but out here we only got fishermen, pilots, maybe some divers or boaters once in awhile. Nobody cared much about offshore lights. I'm as surprised as anyone that this one is being saved."

Facing page: Shining brightly through the misty twilight air, Harbor of Refuge Lighthouse is the first beacon mariners encounter as they navigate the treacherous route up Delaware Bay.

Above: A reflection from the lens room of Harbor of Refuge Lighthouse falls on the pensive face of the tower's last officer-in-charge, Angelo Rigazio. His return to the station in 2001, twenty-eight years after its automation, aroused mixed feelings. "It wasn't so glorious being a lightkeeper in those early days. You wondered what you'd done to deserve the duty. There were a hundred things more exciting."

The initial preservation steps affirmed the critical service the lighthouse has provided to shipping, since its construction in 1926, as well as its place in Delaware Bay maritime history. But simply saving the tower isn't enough for Trapani and his comrades in the Delaware Bay & River Lighthouse Foundation. They want to preserve the human story, too, for the lighthouse was once a home as well as an aid for ships. The people who posed stiffly in front of lighthouses for nineteenth-century portraits actually lived the lighthouse life. So did the later Coast Guard lightkeepers. Trapani wants their story told, and Angelo Rigazio is among the living storytellers.

The lock on the iron door of Harbor of Refuge Lighthouse gave way against years of disuse and swung wide with an arthritic screech. The two men stepped inside and surveyed the remains. The tower was all but gutted and would require hundreds of hours of hard restoration work, paid for largely by public and corporate generosity. Rigazio paced the circular rooms and climbed from deck to deck, mentally refurnishing the place for Trapani, who was eager to know how the lighthouse looked in its last manned years. Restoring the interior to the 1960s period of Coast Guard occupation will address a long-neglected chapter in lighthouse history. It will also offer a small tribute to the modern generation of lighthouse keepers, who succeeded those of the old U.S. Lighthouse Service in 1939 and ushered in the age of modern navigational technology and automation. Coast Guard keepers struggled to tend lighthouses in an era of change, when the click and hum of automatic devices slowly began to silence the tread of footsteps up the spiral stairs.

"I'm not the typical lighthouse keeper people imagine," said Rigazio. "Most of us who served as keepers in the Coast Guard years weren't."

No one pictures a twenty-one-year-old Italian kid, fresh out of machinist-mate school in 1971, working on a lighthouse. Cleaning the priceless optic with "government-issue Windex" and eating meals of spaghetti and baked ziti, punctuated by snacks of Fritos and Pepsi, doesn't connect with the traditional image of the old lightkeeper. "Mooning" passing Navy ships doesn't fit the stereotype either. But these are among the treasured memories of Rigazio and men like him. They got ashore one week out of three, not by rowing miles over uncertain seas, but hauled aloft on a rope beneath the drone of helicopter blades. The circulating libraries and detailed diaries of the early keepers were traded for radio and TV; the whittling and fashioning ships in bottles were swapped for card games and girlie magazines.

Rigazio's first impressions of the lighthouse when he arrived in June 1972 were bittersweet. He'd joined the Coast Guard for adventure, for the excitement of patrolling the coasts, rescuing the unfortunate, policing the seaways.

"'Pack your seabag,' the detailing officer at Cape May told me. 'You're going to Harbor of Refuge.' 'What's that?' I asked, because I really didn't know there was duty like this."

Dropped down to the lonely breakwater tower from a helicopter, with all his worldly possessions in a one bag, he soon discovered the monotony of the daily work and the claustrophobia of confinement on a stump of concrete and metal miles at sea. Four men were assigned to the lighthouse, but only three were in residence at once, sometimes just two, depending on the leave rotation. They shared a kitchen, a bathroom, a bunkroom, and the everyday lightkeeping tasks. The food allowance was sixty dollars a month per man, pooled by the entire crew. Whoever went on leave when the larder ran spare bought groceries in the commissary at Cape May Coast Guard Station—fifty pounds of potatoes, five gallons of Ragu pasta sauce, two dozen loaves of bread, five pounds of butter, ten packs of hot dogs, maybe some cake mixes, and Oreos and Twinkies.

Rigazio's days were twenty-four-hour tedium punctuated with moments of frenzy. Weather reports were radioed to Cape May six times day. The logbook tracked the amount of water and fuel used. Once a week the light was cleaned and the fog trumpets checked. If the light on the opposite breakwater couldn't be seen, the foghorns were started. If ice or snow built up on the lantern windows, they were scraped clean. In summer the greenhead flies assailed the tower, and in fall it was blackflies. Birds met their death against the lantern during migration months and had to be swept away.

Rarely, a storm blew in off the Atlantic and sent fifteen- to twenty-foot waves over the breakwater into the harbor for which the lighthouse had been named. A rogue wave would sometimes slam the tower with a sudden boom and shudder as sea met metal. Winter ice jammed against the tower, cloaking its base and the 1.5-mile-long breakwater in a frozen glistening mantle. Summer thunderheads crossed the bay and unleashed bolts of lightning on the lonely edifice.

"We'd get in the center of the tower during thunderstorms and wait it out. When you're the tallest object around and made of metal, too, you're going to get hit,

Perched at the end of the longest breakwater in the United States, Harbor of Refuge Lighthouse is accessible only by boat. During its manned years, keepers' daily lives were ruled by the uncertainty of weather. "Seas running" meant no boat could dock and shore leave was cancelled. Men were sometimes marooned on the tower for weeks.

no question. There'd be a loud crack and pop," Rigazio said, clapping his hands for effect, "Then the electricity would go out, and a few seconds later the backup generators kicked on to power the light."

One summer day a body floated near the lighthouse. A young girl had drowned while swimming at nearby Cape Henlopen. The lightkeepers pulled her from the bay and administered CPR, but it was too late. Rigazio slept poorly for several nights, his dreams haunted by a tangled mat of wet hair, pale, wrinkled skin, and vacant eyes. Reminders of how dangerous the sea could be weren't usually so graphic.

There were pleasant days, too. The men fished off the rocks using squid for bait. Dinners of striped bass, tautog, and bluefish were common in the summer months. Lobsters were tossed up to the men by friendly fishermen. Beer was handed up as well and kept cold in the freshwater tanks in the lighthouse. If the Coast Guard ship *Sassafras* was sighted heading in with an inspector on board, the brew was hidden in the rocks, as no alcohol was permitted on the light. The *Sassafras* also brought fresh water to be pumped into the cedar tanks on the first deck and diesel fuel to run the station.

The radio was the crew's lifeline to shore. They reported to Cape May every four hours with the weather, but they also called in when an emergency arose or something was needed. Occasionally, the men played "Radio Chess" with the crews of other lighthouses in the bay—Fourteen Foot Bank, Ship John Shoal, Miah Maull, Brandywine Shoal, Elbow of Cross Ledge. Two crews tried to checkmate each other while the rest listened in and planned their turns at play. More personal communications took place by radio, too. Like all married lightkeepers, Rigazio conversed with his wife in Cape May every few days. He communicated by proxy, first sending a message to the radio operator who sent it on to Darlene Rigazio, who then came back with her reply. Everyone eavesdropped, of course. The couple had code words for privacy, but there was always teasing afterwards. When Mrs. Rigazio discovered she was pregnant, she radioed Cape May saying, "Tell Angelo the rabbit died."

All of this was sometimes said in the eighteen-second pauses between the foghorns' deafening blasts. The twin trumpets faced seaward from the outside wall of the third deck and were powered by compressors on the ground floor. As chief engineer, it was Rigazio's job to keep them honking, a task he approached with ambivalence, for foghorns in good repair meant unending noise during bouts of foul weather. There was no peace

on the third deck when the horns were going, but the men knew the racket was necessary and a charity for seamen. The noise could be heard about eight miles at sea, depending on the thickness of the air and the direction of wind. On the lighthouse, however, it was hazardous to the ears, and each man had to wear custom-made earplugs.

The light was maintained 365 days a year in all manner of weather, regardless of personal needs and desires. Men missed their wives and children on holidays, birthdays, or anniversaries, giving total allegiance to the light.

In many respects, the Coast Guard era was no different than the days of the old "wickies," the nickname given to lightkeepers prior to electrification when oil lamps illuminated the beacon and wicks had to be trimmed. Yet in other respects, life on the breakwater lighthouse was far more challenging and dangerous in its early years.

The lighthouse perches on the longest breakwater in the United States and the third longest in the world, affording it a protective view over the port of Lewes and making it a vital link in the chain of navigational aids guarding Delaware Bay. Storms accost it, ice grinds and gnaws its concrete base, and thousands of vessels, from small recreational boats to mega-tankers, seek its guiding light each year.

The first sentinel here was a temporary thirty-foot frustum of planks built in 1901. In no way did it acknowledge the grandeur of the breakwater it marked or the ferocity of its seaward side. The *Annual Report* of the Lighthouse Board for 1903 detailed its fate: "The severe storm beginning on September 16, 1903, during which the wind was reported to have attained a velocity of 85 miles an hour, carried away the temporary frame light-tower and washed from the wharf into the harbor a 2,000 pound fogbell and fogbell striking machine."

A galvanized steel skeleton tower provided a beacon until 1908 when a grander, caisson-style guardian was commissioned. Like a castle turret, it rose fifty-two feet high with hexagonal wooden walls and handsome lead-colored appointments—a beauty locals called the "Belle of the Bay." But wood and seawater seldom make a happy marriage. The logbook soberly recorded each assault:

January 4, 1918—Breakwater froze up. . . .

April 10, 1918—Storm did considerable damage to the station. . . . Broken lighthouse foundation shifted the big light about two inches. . . .

February 5, 1920—Northeast storm did damage . . . washed everything off the dock . . . wind and

"Red for danger" is the warning of many harbor and channel lights. Lightkeepers were ever vigilant of Harbor of Refuge's important red sectors, which marked the treacherous Hen & Chickens Shoals at the entrance to the bay and the Brown Shoals to the northwest of the breakwater. When the reflection was just right, it even marked the stairwell door leading down to their circular quarters.

Rainbow-like artifacts of the tower's modern VRB-25 lamp shimmer through its plastic prismatic dome. A 1,000-watt bulb provides the light source, visible twenty miles. "It works on principles similar to an old Fresnel lens," says former keeper Angelo Rigazio, "Only it's more durable and compact."

high seas moved the lighthouse about two inches on its foundation . . . no water to drink. . . .

In 1921, the final blow came when a hurricane wheeled up the coast and slammed the Delaware Bay. One man made it safely ashore. The other was found the day after the storm, tied to a broken post. When the lighthouse foundered, he had tethered himself to the splintered spar in hopes the waves would not take him. No doubt, the account has been embellished with drama over the years as it was told to every keeper newly assigned to the current lighthouse, built in 1926. Such stories provide the measure of humility needed to live with the sea just outside one's door.

The lock on the lighthouse door clicked shut, and the motor launch pulled away from Harbor of Refuge in the late afternoon, headed back to Lewes. Rigazio stood facing the stern, watching the tower at Harbor of Refuge grow smaller and smaller in the distance, and he remembered that it was celebrating its seventy-fifth birthday this year. How good to come back and visit with an old friend who's looking well and whose purpose is still apparent.

"I wouldn't want to live here again—those days were tough. Better to remember than relive. But I'm glad it'll be cared for—it deserves that."

Trapani grasped the wall of the pilothouse with one hand and pointed to nearby Cape Henlopen with the

other. The sun had begun its descent, laying down a pink patina on the dunes where the first lighthouse in Delaware, Cape Henlopen Light, was built in 1767. It stood watch 159 years—more than 58,000 nights—before the sea toppled it in 1926, about the same time the present Harbor of Refuge Lighthouse flashed its first rays over the bay. Six lighthouses have stood on this restive stretch of Delaware shore. Four now lie in the ocean.

At the dock in Lewes, Rigazio turned for one last look at the lighthouse, a reassuring glance across three miles of water and three decades of memory. Trapani looked as well and sighed, as if he knew what Rigazio was thinking.

"It'll take money and hard work, but we'll do it."

Rigazio nodded. Old keeper and new keeper stood together, joining perspectives and considering the huge task ahead. There is no formula for rescuing an aging lighthouse; each one must undergo its own rejuvenation. Politics prescribes a course for historic preservation while funding steers a timeline for progress. There are engineering surveys and structural analyses and abatement studies, short-term plans and long-term plans. But what truly saves a lighthouse are passionate and resolute people.

The baritone horn of the Cape May–Lewes ferry sounded as the boat eased away from the auto gate next to the pilot station. Within minutes the huge vessel, its

The Delaware Bay can be clement or cruel. Unpredictable weather vindicates the presence of seven major lighthouses over a distance of about fifty miles. For summer ferry travelers, however, the lighthouses seem mere postcard decorations on the pleasant crossing between Lewes and Cape May. "People don't realize that nothing lies between Harbor of Refuge Light and Spain, except 3,000 miles of unfettered ocean," says former lightkeeper and author Stephen Jones, who was assigned to the tower during the damaging storm that slammed the bay in March 1962. "Let them come back on a bad day and see the other face of the bay."

belly filled with cars and its rails lined with passengers, was passing Harbor of Refuge Lighthouse. People crowded on the port side to admire the handsome tower rising minaret-like from the breakwater. Cameras came out of bags to capture smiling faces and the wonderfully nautical backdrop. Some people waved and shouted a greeting, as if they thought at any moment a lightkeeper might appear and wave back.

If Trapani and Rigazio have their way, that just may happen.

An array of solar panels on the south side of the weather deck attests to modernization at Harbor of Refuge Lighthouse. During its manned years, human hands tended the light on a daily basis. Now completely self-sufficient, it requires checks by Coast Guard maintenance crews about every three months.

Small against the girth of his former home, Angelo Rigazio looks down from the caisson deck thirty feet above sea. His bittersweet reunion with the lighthouse is shared by nearly all of its past keepers. "It was a blessing to get off the light in 1973 and go ashore for good, but it meant something different for the lighthouse," he says. Sealed windows, rust, and peeling paint are the downside of automation.

CHAPTER I

Kindling a Flame

Left: *The tranquil moonlit waters of the Chesapeake Bay belie its perilous course. Colonists quickly realized that prosperity from the commerce this and other waterways afforded would come at great risk. Lighthouses were desperately needed, but nearly two centuries would pass before the first sentinels lit the New World. Sandy Point Shoal Lighthouse near Annapolis was not built until 1858, during the heyday of lighthouse construction in America.*

Above: *Scarred by tempest and turmoil, the rugged walls of Sandy Hook, the Mid-Atlantic's first lighthouse, were constructed of rubblestone to form a truncated octagonal cone. This functional design by New York architect and merchant, Isaac Conro, was copied throughout the colonies and reflected the frugal and sturdy character of the nation's early settlers.*

Our country is much intersected by navigable waters.
Thomas Jefferson,
"Notes on the State of Virginia," 1780

In the winter of 1607, 105 hopeful English colonists set sail for America. After a voyage of eighteen weeks, they sighted their destination, a scattering of forested islands and sandy beaches burnished by the warm April sun. Navigating the shoal-ridden coast wasn't easy, but the land seemed rich and wondrous. Dogwood and wild strawberries dappled the hills, birds rose from the grasslands in winged brigades, sweet oysters lay hidden in the tidal flats. And so many fish congregated in the waters it seemed they might be caught by hand.

Two great capes guarded the seventeen-mile-wide mouth of a shallow but vast bay the natives called Chesepiooc. Little did the wayfarers know they had entered the largest estuary in North America, an expanse of some 2,500 square miles. Grateful to be near journey's end, they dropped anchor on the southern headland, which they named for their beloved Prince Henry, son of King James I. Stumbling wearily up the dunes, they fell to their knees in a prayer of thanks. The light that had guided them was faith, for no actual beacons yet stood on American shores. It would be more than two centuries, during which thousands of hopeful pioneers would arrive and a war would bring independence, before a true lighthouse shone from Cape Henry.

A year after the Jamestown settlement was founded, Henry Hudson explored these same shores, admiring the Mid-Atlantic's coastal beauty as he navigated the *Half Moon* northward and into a large, deep bay. The ingress gave way to a fine, wide river walled by magnificent peaks and extending more than one hundred miles into the interior. The river would later bear his name, and its treacherous course be rendered more welcome by a necklace of lights draped along both sides of its twisting course, beginning at Albany and ending with beams over New York Bay and Long Island Sound.

Less than year after Hudson's travels, Samuel Argall went looking for the Virginia settlement and accidentally sailed into another fine bay that he named in honor of Lord de la Warr, Thomas West, governor of Virginia. The broad estuary lured settlers up a winding river, which opened into a region ripe for a port city to carry away the riches of fur traders and farmers. Philadelphia would handle a panoply of cargoes in the years ahead, and its merchants would string a line of guiding beacons all the way to Cape May.

These important bodies of water—Chesapeake Bay,

Hudson River, New York Bay, Long Island Sound, Delaware Bay—and the many inland waterways feeding them became the new land's liquid highways that would direct settlement and commerce along the mid-Atlantic coast for the next four centuries. Hundreds of lighthouses in a variety of architectural forms would rise along their shores to answer the needs of shipping. A singular department of government would evolve to build and maintain them. But first, the colonies had to establish themselves, grow, and develop their ports.

Glimmers of Light

Despite struggles to survive in an unfamiliar landscape, colonies took root beyond Virginia and drew hordes of hopeful European immigrants. Crowded and economically strained, England looked to America for relief and opportunity and found both in the Mid-Atlantic. The region offered good farmland, mild winters, and many waterways into the interior. By 1700, English settlements thrived throughout the region. A town rose up at the mouth of the Potomac River and a fort stood at Old Point Comfort, protected by the large natural harbor of Hampton Roads. Puritans founded Annapolis at the mouth of the Severn River; Dutch and Swedes settled parts of Delaware and New York; and a placid Quaker named William Penn bought 50,000 square miles of sylvan land from the native Delaware Indians.

Almost daily, shiploads of immigrants arrived and the bounty of mid-Atlantic riches departed—furs, dried fish, tobacco, wheat, and other crops—to be exchanged for goods needed in the burgeoning colonies. Even so, no lighthouses stood anywhere along the American coast. There was plenty of commerce between the old and new worlds to warrant building navigational aids, but England parsimoniously ignored its unlit colonies. They were expensive enough to maintain and a bit arrogant as well. Why give them lighthouses when many English shores still remained dark?

In 1713, Massachusetts Bay colony merchants and shipmasters began vigorously petitioning the British General Court for a lighthouse at the entrance to Boston Harbor. Barely sixty feet tall, the rubblestone tower on Little Brewster Island shone a light for the first time in September 1716, its beacon produced by a chandelier of tallow candles. Though feeble, it gave guidance to vessels arriving at night or in foul weather. Construction and maintenance funds and the keeper's salary were raised by a duty collected from ships entering and leaving the harbor.

By 1760, three more lights were established in New

Patriarch of American lighthouses, the handsome sentinel at Sandy Hook went into service in 1764 on a long, narrow peninsula jutting toward New York Harbor. Owners of the land where it was to be built demanded £750 for the small tract, despite arguments from New York merchants that the soil was poor and would support no crops for the lightkeeper. Perhaps as a compromise, the deed provided for free-run pasturage of two cows and a stipulation that "no public house for the selling of strong liquors" could be built on the site.

Facing page and above: Like its sister sentry at Sandy Hook, the Cape Henlopen Lighthouse was of simple, sturdy design, only taller. The obvious difference was location. The beach at Cape Henlopen was in constant flux under the intrusion of currents off the Delaware Bay. While the tower at Sandy Hook stood firm, Cape Henlopen Lighthouse was threatened by erosion throughout its career. It succumbed in 1926 only days after this photo (facing page) was taken.

England and one in the young colony of Georgia, but the Mid-Atlantic continued to lay dark despite its flourishing commerce and the constant pleas of merchants and shipmasters. Edmund Andros, colonial governor of New York, saw the need for a lighthouse at Sandy Hook as early as 1680 and suggested to Governor Philip Carteret of New Jersey that "sea-marks for shipping" be placed on the sandspit. New Jersey bore the unsavory sobriquet "Graveyard of Ships." The approach to New York Bay had claimed numerous vessels and was marked by a single crude beacon—a lantern hung in an elm tree on Staten Island. Sandy Hook, pointing to New York like a crooked finger, seemed the best location for a lighthouse, but nearly a century would pass before a sentinel was built there.

The residents of northern New Jersey, knowing the peril of their shoreline and fearing attack by the French, who were then at war with Britain, began maintaining a

simple fire beacon on the Navesink Highlands. It consisted of a signal system on a tall pole, possibly one hundred feet high, "using large hoisted balls in daytime and lighted kegs of oil at night." Supposedly, it could be seen in New York City fifteen miles away. By this time, wrecking—the salvage of shipwrecked cargo and sunken vessels—had arisen as a viable business along the New Jersey coast, further suggesting the need for an aid to navigation at Sandy Hook. As the port of New York grew and the skeletons of wrecked ships piled up, merchants agitated for a lighthouse. An article in the February 1757 *New York Post Boy* stressed the need for a sentinel. Later in the year, a shipwreck off southern Long Island caused public uproar and led to a chafing editorial in the *Pennsylvania Gazette*, which blamed the tragedy on lack of a lighthouse on Sandy Hook.

Costly shipping losses early in 1761 and a petition signed by forty-three merchants spurred the Colonial Assembly of New York to authorize a lottery to fund the lighthouse. (Lotteries were common at this time and a viable way of raising money for public projects.) The following year, enough money had been raised to buy four acres at the tip of the sandspit. A year later a second lottery, combined with a duty levied on passing ships, accrued the remaining funds needed to start construction. Isaac Conro, an architect, builder, and merchant from New York City, was hired to construct the lighthouse "eight chains and fifty links" (about five hundred feet) from the high-water mark. He chose a nine-story, 103-foot-tall, octagonal design of rubblestone. A wooden staircase spiraled to an iron lantern covered with hammered copper. The lantern enclosed the lighting fixture described by the *New York Mercury* as "48 Oil Blazes." New York Lighthouse, as it was then called, was illuminated for the first time on the night of June 11, 1764. The cost for the project was a little over $5,000.

Inspired by the success at Sandy Hook, merchants and shipowners in Philadelphia turned their thoughts to a lighthouse for Cape Henlopen, a mercurial stretch of sand hills at the southern entrance to the Delaware Bay. The cape overlooked the dreaded Hen and Chicken Shoals. These sandbars caught many vessels, including Hudson's *Half Moon*, which grazed the shoals with her rudder while passing through in August 1609. Hudson wrote in his log that none but the smallest vessels should sail near this cape and advance into the bay only after repeated soundings.

As with other colonial lighthouses, a lottery funded Cape Henlopen Light. In September 1763, enough money had been collected for the General Assembly of Pennsylvania to position a stone lighthouse and several buoys in the bay and river leading to Philadelphia. Land was obtained from the heirs of William Penn, and granite quarried from Wilmington was sent by barge to Cape Henlopen. The tower was completed in 1765.

The Cape Henlopen light was similar to its sister sentry at Sandy Hook but had cost three times as much. Worse, it stood less than a quarter mile from sea and perilously close to a ridge of unstable dunes that would torment it for most of its career. Yet Cape Henlopen Lighthouse was sturdy—the loftiest structure of its day south of Philadelphia—and distinguished by a state-of-the-art illuminating apparatus of whale-oil lamps. Beside the tower stood a lightkeeper's house, built from bricks that had arrived as ballast on English ships. A stable housed oxen for hauling oil and supplies over the sand between the lighthouse and the wharf at Lewes.

In 1718, representatives of shipowners and merchants in the Chesapeake Bay area approached Governor Alexander Spotswood of Virginia about building a lighthouse at Cape Henry. Fire baskets burned along the cape from time to time, but pirates and "mooncussers" often moved them to deceive ships and profit from salvage of the wrecks. Numerous petitions for a lighthouse failed over the years, but in 1772 work finally began. Four thousand tons of stone were shipped to the site, which was not far from where in 1608 the first Jamestown settlers had raised their cross of gratitude for a safe voyage. The lighthouse foundation had been dug and a few stones laid when funds ran out. Additional money was requested, but before it could be allocated, the Revolution began and work was abandoned. Sand surreptitiously covered the piles of undressed granite and filled in the foundation of the would-be lighthouse. The project was forgotten while a nascent nation suffered the pangs of birth.

Revolution

As cries for independence reverberated through the colonies, eleven lighthouses were on the beam—seven in New England, two in the Mid-Atlantic, and two in the South—and plans were afoot to build more. In addition, a number of minor aids, such as fog cannons, buoys, and spindles, were in use. Americans were proud of the civility their coastline exhibited, especially at a time when most European colonies lacked navigational aids of any sort.

With a growing feeling of separateness from the mother country, it would seem that patriots might have fervently defended their lighthouses during the Revolution. They did not. The towers quickly emerged as tangible symbols of British rule and became favored targets of patriots' aggression, as well as pawns in the powerplays between warring forces. Americans saw them as aids for the invading British, while the British often considered them excellent staging points for attacks on important ports.

Realizing that British warships needed the lighthouse at Sandy Hook Lighthouse to guide them safely into New York Harbor, patriots decided to dismantle it. In March 1776, Colonel George Taylor of the Monmouth County militia led a group of men to the lighthouse and removed its illuminating apparatus, plus its tools, the oil supply, and anything else that could aid the British in relighting the tower. A small squadron of British naval ships anchored off Sandy Hook shortly thereafter. In need of provisions, the commander of the British squadron began sending parties of men ashore near the lighthouse to hunt and fetch water. The New Jersey militia delighted in harassing the men. The New York *Journal* reported in April that a group of British seamen "had gotten into the upper room of the lighthouse, where they were carousing; when a party of New Jersey Militia surprised them, taking away the lower part of the stairs, made them prisoners, burned their boat, and filled up the well." The incident so angered the British commander, he ordered his men to capture the lighthouse and secure it from further attack. A makeshift beacon was placed in the tower and several warships were anchored near it.

In May 1776, American forces under the command of Lieutenant Colonel Benjamin Tupper attempted to destroy the beacon at Sandy Hook by firing cannon shot into its walls. They were surprised to find the tower stood firm, "the walls so thick as to make no impression," Tupper later wrote in a letter to George Washington. Another attack in July also failed to bring down the lighthouse, and four subsequent raids in the next year fared no better. Realizing the near impenetrability of the structure, the British proceeded to construct a stone breast work around the base and cut portholes in the walls of the first floor for cannon barrels to project. These changes made the lighthouse even more defensible to American attack.

Later in the war, the light tower at Sandy Hook provided asylum for Loyalists from New Jersey and New

Attempts to destroy the lighthouse at Sandy Hook during the Revolutionary War were unsuccessful, due in large part to its impenetrability. A window alcove in the tower attests to its thick walls.

York. Their encampment at the base of the tower was called Refugeetown and the lighthouse was dubbed Refugee Tower. These British sympathizers, calling themselves by such names as the Jersey Volunteers and Pine Robbers, launched raids on local villages and sold their contraband at Sandy Hook. Among the groups were the Black Pioneers, a group of runaway slaves the British had armed and ordered to take revenge on their masters.

At Cape Henlopen, the lighthouse keeper was joined by a lookout in the spring of 1776 to watch for the approach of British vessels and warn the mainland if he felt an attack was at hand. Buoys were pulled from the Delaware Bay to discourage British ships from entering, and harbor pilots, who assisted incoming vessels, were cautioned not to help them. By summer, the Delaware militia had posted some one hundred men to guard the lighthouse. But this small force was not there in April

1777 when British crewmen dispatched from the man-of-war *Roebuck* came ashore at Cape Henlopen in a longboat and demanded the lighthouse keeper give them his cows. He refused. When the men were out of sight, the keeper rounded up his stock and herded them into the pines. The British returned and set fire to the empty lighthouse's wooden stairway and lantern. The entire structure was gutted and spent the remainder of the war dark and uninhabited.

Thus, the Mid-Atlantic's two colonial lighthouses survived the Revolution, but at great cost. Both were damaged, and their proud service as sentries had been stained by political upheaval. The new nation was penniless and quarrelsome, its land scorched and trampled, and its citizens weary. Though peace came with the surrender at Yorktown, it would be a decade before the fledging government mustered the resources to rebuild and expand its chain of navigational beacons.

EARLY ILLUMINATION: CANDLES AND LAMPWICKS

America's first beacons were simple pole lights fitted with baskets in which bales of pitched-soaked ocum (rags) were burned. The earliest of these beacons stood on Point Allerton in Massachusetts to serve the young port of Boston. Later, similar beacons were exhibited at various important spots along the coast, including the Highlands at Navesink, New Jersey; Cape Henry at the mouth of the Chesapeake Bay; even an elm tree on Staten Island. Their purpose was twofold—to warn residents in the event of an attack and to guide ships at night or in foul weather.

With the construction of the first lighthouses, enclosed lanterns allowed for more sophisticated illuminants. A chandelier of tallow candles was installed in the Boston Lighthouse in 1716. The keeper was careful to prevent tallow from soaking into the wooden floor of the lantern, creating a fire hazard. By the mid 1700s, oil lamps were in use at most lighthouses. There was no standard design at first, but most of these lamps had a cotton-rope wick feeding into a reservoir of fish oil, seal oil, or whale oil. There were no glass chimneys on the lamps, and they produced a feeble, smoky light and a foul odor.

Pan lamps were in use when Sandy Hook Light was completed in 1764. These lamps consisted of enclosed trays of oil in which multiple wicks were suspended. They could burn for an entire night without refueling, making them ideal for lighthouses. Sandy Hook's lantern had two large pan lamps, hung from the ceiling, with a total of forty-eight oil blazes. Round versions were called compass lamps and were used well into the nineteenth century by a number of lighthouses, as well as on lightships.

Cape Henry Lighthouse, lit in 1792, used bucket lamps. These resembled large metal watering cans with many spouts. A thick rope wick fed down each spout into the oil can, which could hold about two gallons of oil and would burn throughout the night. The keeper's work consisted primarily of keeping the wicks trimmed during the night, periodically cleaning soot and smoke from the lantern windows, and keeping the oil from congealing in cold weather.

About this same time, French physicist Francois-Pierre Ami Argand invented a much-improved lamp. Its radical new feature was a hollow wick that burned clearer, brighter, and cleaner than flat or rope wicks. The circular wick was encased in a double metal tube, and the flame enclosed by a glass chimney, allowing it to burn steadier and receive additional oxygen. An oil reservoir fueled the wick via a thin, curved tube. A single Argand lamp equaled seven candles. In 1784, a silver-coated parabolic reflector to amplify the light was added. By 1800, Argand lamps were in use in American lighthouses and remained popular until 1812 when a modified version, patented by Winslow Lewis of Cape Cod, replaced it.

Lewis's "Magnifying & Reflecting Lantern" attempted to improve on Argand's work by adding a magnifier of convex, green bottle glass to each lamp. A tree of lamps and magnifiers, arranged in circles piggyback-style, comprised the illuminating apparatus. Though Lewis's idea made sense, he lacked the knowledge and skill to make it work effectively. His glass optics were of poor quality, as were the reflectors, which were more spherical in shape than parabolic. The entire system did little, if anything, to improve lighthouse illumination. Lewis attempted to improve the design over the years, but it remained problematic and inferior to systems then used in Europe. His political influence enabled him to supply U.S. lighthouses with optics for some forty years and shut out competitors. His lighting system survived until the second half of the nineteenth century when prism lenses were adopted.

The aging, but bright, lantern of Sandy Hook Lighthouse has used a variety of illuminants. The first consisted of two whale-oil pan lamps hung from the ceiling with twenty-four wicks inserted into each pan. These burned all night without refueling, but the wicks had to be trimmed often, and fumes and soot created considerable cleaning work for the keeper.

CHAPTER 2

Civilizing the Shore

Left: *The new nation demonstrated its international status and civility by assuming control of the twelve colonial lighthouses in 1789 and authorizing construction of new lights. By the time the Lighthouse Board took control of the lighthouses in 1851, more than two hundred sentinels stood watch in the United States and cutting-edge technology in illumination had taken hold with the adoption of prismatic lenses.*

Above: *The first official public works project authorized by the first Congress of the United States provided for the construction of a lighthouse at Cape Henry, Virginia. Its original wooden stairway was replaced by cast-iron stairs in the mid-nineteenth century, but the brickwork of the first lighthouse still stands strong.*

One of the noblest characteristics of our great nation is her generosity, and this trait is most widely evidenced by her conduct in regard to the numerous lights and aids to navigation along her coast.
Joanna R. Nichols,
"The United States Lighthouse Establishment,"
Frank Leslie's Popular Monthly, September 1896

On August 7, 1789, our nation's first Congress in its first session passed the Ninth Act, a public works measure that put twelve lighthouses under the control of the new federal government. The states agreed to transfer, and all the lights were in federal hands by 1793. Eleven lighthouses had been built in the colonial period, and two more had gone into service at Great Point, Nantucket, in 1784 and Newburyport, Massachusetts, in 1788. However, Boston Light had been completely destroyed during the war and only a pile of rubble remained where it had stood in the harbor.

The Ninth Act provided for "necessary support, maintenance and repairs of all lighthouses, beacons, buoys, and public piers erected, placed, or sunk before the passage of this Act, at the entrance of, or within any bay, inlet, harbor, or port of the United States." The Secretary of the Treasury Alexander Hamilton was charged with overseeing these affairs and was the first official head of the United States Lighthouse Establishment.

Hamilton went to work immediately, placing each lighthouse under the control of the collector of customs for the port it guarded. The beacons at Cape Henlopen and Sandy Hook, already relighted, were assessed for repairs and their lightkeepers approved for duty. Hamilton urged Congress to dispense with dues levied on passing ships, believing the move would encourage commerce and that the Treasury Department could handle the financial responsibility of navigational aids entirely on its own. Additionally, he began the onerous task of building more lighthouses.

Sturdy Stone Towers

At Cape Henry, where vestiges of pre-war construction lay beneath the sand, land was ceded to the federal government in November 1789 for Virginia's first lighthouse and the nation's premier public works project. The contract went to New York bricklayer John McComb, Jr. and carefully spelled out his responsibilities and the details of the lighthouse's construction. Very much like its sister sentries at Cape Henlopen and Sandy Hook, the Cape Henry Lighthouse was utter simplicity—strong and

Both photos: *Cape Henry Lighthouse was built to be functional and durable. Plain windows bring light into each course, including the small watchroom where a narrow ladder leads to the lantern. Lack of ornamentation affirms the new government's frugal purse and humble character.*

A long-awaited beacon for the entrance to the Chesapeake Bay, ninety-foot Cape Henry Lighthouse was built by New York mason John McComb, Jr., following a design similar to several other colonial lighthouses. By this time American architects knew enough about lighthouse construction to include a lightning rod in the plans and wire netting to ward off birds. The thick walls of the old Cape Henry tower have survived storms, war, and even an earthquake.

FOG SONGS

From a lighthouse beyond the harbor's mouth, a foghorn is heard at regular
intervals moaning like a mournful whale in labor.
Eugene O'Neill, "Long Day's Journey into Night," 1940

Not every task at a lighthouse was devoted solely to the beacon. There were sundry other jobs, not the least of which was tending the fog signal. When the air grew murky and the light failed to show its maximum distance, sound became the mariner's guide.

Cannons were used at some New England and West Coast lighthouses, but in the Mid-Atlantic bells were the earliest sound signals. Their clarion tones carried well, and it was up to the keepers to ring them by hand. At some stations where poor visibility was prevalent this was a seemingly endless task. It helped to have a family to assist with the work. Visitors often considered the task a novelty and were graciously permitted to attend to it. Dogs were taught to yank the bell clapper rope. One clever keeper rigged up a line to the bell striker, threaded it through his bedroom window, and lay in bed at night ringing the bell with his toes.

In 1880, Thimble Shoal Lighthouse at the entrance to Hampton Roads was given two fogbells, one on the north side of the tower and one on the south side, to signal to ships from both directions. By this time automatic bell strikers were in service at most lighthouses, freeing keepers from the monotonous manual chore. The work then consisted of winding up weights suspended in the bell tower. As the weights descended, they powered a clockworks mechanism that actuated the striker.

About 1850, a Canadian music teacher developed the first steam-powered fog signal when he mounted a whistle on a steam boiler. Sirens and horns were adapted to steam engines a short time later. The familiar two-tone "be-ooohh" of the diaphone horn came along by 1870 and the multi-toned diaphragm horn a decade later. These three types of signals—whistles, horns, and sirens—became the standards of fog signaling in the late nineteenth century. For the keepers, there was considerable labor involved in the operation of all of these devices. A sturdy fog house joined the outbuildings; black horns protruded from the seaward walls, and coal-fired boilers inside produced the steam that rendered a station's signature honk, screech, or whistle. The boilers were cantankerous about starting and were challenging to maintain. Coal had to be shoveled and the machinery coddled. Breakdowns were frequent, and bells had to be kept as backups.

Government researchers continually experimented with sound signals to improve warnings to mariners and ease the work of lightkeepers. In 1921, they developed an unusual hygroscope using human hair, and a prototype was installed in Baltimore Harbor and at Lambert Point near Norfolk. Each consisted of a pigtail attached to the electrical switch of a 2,000-pound fogbell. Researchers knew that hair responds to humidity by contracting and to dryness by stretching. The pigtail would contract when the fog rolled in and open the switch to actuate the bell striker. Once dryer air returned, the hair would stretch and close the switch. The device was clever and economical, costing $1,300 to develop and a mere eight dollars per month to operate.

Unfortunately, no one had considered how an artificial fog would affect the apparatus. The occasion of its undoing was the dedication ceremony for the Francis Scott Key Memorial. The day was sunny and clear, but fireboats were rocketing streams over Baltimore Harbor in celebration. Moisture drifted across the water and the pigtail began to contract. In the middle of a stirring speech by President Warren Harding, the recalcitrant bell loudly came to life, sending its urgent but unneeded clangs over the fogless water and drowning out the president's voice.

When electricity was successfully adapted to power fog signals in the early twentieth century, it was the keepers who cheered loudest. Backbreaking work and worry was finally replaced by a flip of a switch.

To the shipmaster, the various sounds of fog signals compose a lifesaving symphony. Keepers and their families dutifully adapted to the intermittent cacophony, pausing in their conversations when bells bonged, horns blared, or sirens shrieked. They slept with cotton in their ears and reminded themselves that this was benevolent noise. It meant the seaways were safer in the fog. But not everyone finds fog signals so pleasing. Great Captain Island Lighthouse received a new fog siren in 1905 to differentiate it from the many other sounds emanating from the busy waterway of western Long Island Sound. Nearby residents of Connecticut and New York protested that the noise kept them awake at night. A local newspaper reporter penned lines of purple prose about the unpopular signal, likening it to "an army of panthers . . . roar of a thousand bulls . . . wail of a lost soul . . . moan of a bottomless pit . . . and groan of a disabled elevator." The Lighthouse Board refused to change the siren, however, for the sound was a treacherous stretch of water.

Today's fog signals consist primarily of plastic/acrylic horns that actuate automatically when the air thickens. The horns are small, compact, durable, dependable, and practically carefree. Laser sensors measure visibility and trip the actuator when needed. Electrical hookups or solar batteries supply power, and Coast Guard maintenance teams periodically check the automatic setups. Seldom do the horns require work. The mournful nasal wails these modern fog signals send over the water are still important for navigation.

A variety of contrivances were tried by the lighthouse service to penetrate fog, but none as melodious and beloved as the fogbell. Bells were inaugurated in 1820 at New England's West Quoddy Lighthouse and quickly became the signal of choice throughout the nation. Early versions had to be struck by hand, but by the 1870s mechanical strikers were in use along with a host of other noisemakers including whistles, sirens, and horns. Though many of the bells have been silenced, fogbell lore echoes with whimsical stories. At some stations lightkeepers boasted of owning "fog dogs" trained to yank the bell clapper ropes when the murk rolled in.

Dominating a bluff at the eastern tip of Long Island, Montauk Point Lighthouse has changed little since its construction in 1797. It represents the American Dream more than any other lighthouse, for until the Statue of Liberty was lighted in 1886, Montauk Point Lighthouse was the first emblem of a new life seen by European immigrants arriving in New York.

functional in design without the slightest hint of ornamentation. Rocks quarried from the Rappahannock River dressed its sturdy stone walls, which were three feet thick at the base. A spiraling wooden staircase led to the wrought-iron lantern in which eight lamps, hanging in two tiers, burned fish oil. The twenty-eight panes of glass were enclosed by a brass wire netting, "so as to preserve the Glass in the lantern from injuries by Hail, or flights of birds in the Night." The copper roof had "electrical conductors to secure it from the effects of Lightning." McComb was paid $15,200 for the project. The ninety-foot octagonal tower of dressed stone, along with

a frame keeper's house, went into service in October 1792. President George Washington personally appointed the first keeper, a local man named Laban Goffigan, who agreed to an annual salary of $266.

As the lamps in Cape Henry Lighthouse were inaugurated with flame, plans were being made to place a beacon on the eastern tip of Long Island at Montauk Point to serve as a landfall for vessels arriving from overseas. Already this point of land bore the nickname "The Fork," for it was where vessels from Europe turned north if bound for New England or south if headed for the Mid-Atlantic. Off the tip of Long Island lay dismal

Shagwong Reef, among other hazards. During bad weather, the full fury of the Atlantic bore down on the point, swallowing as much as three feet of cliff a year. Ezra L'Homendieu, surveyor for the lighthouse, noted that "as the Bank is washed by the sea in storms, we suppose it best to set the building at [a] distance."

The site chosen for the lighthouse was a mound the Montauk Indians called Turtle Hill, some 297 feet inland from the bluff. At such elevation the beacon could easily be seen from east and west, allowing it to serve ships in both directions. Land was purchased in 1793, and two years later, President Washington signed the contract authorizing John McComb, Jr.—the same man who had built Cape Henry Lighthouse—to construct Montauk Point Lighthouse. The one-hundred-foot tower was completed in November 1797, again a near replica of its compatriots at Sandy Hook, Cape Henlopen, and Cape Henry. Lamps and oil arrived several months later, with the beacon's official inception in the spring of 1798. New York State had its first lighthouse, ironically lit on the very spot where the British Navy had kept a bonfire to guide its ships during the Revolution. Montauk Point Lighthouse wore a more peaceful countenance and soon became the symbol of freedom and opportunity for thousands of immigrants pouring into the young United States.

The nation now turned its attention to Long Island Sound, known for years as the "Devil's Belt" and a vital waterway for ships entering and leaving New York from the north. Eatons Neck, a small promontory overlooking the entrance to Huntington Bay, seemed the best place to start. The government bought ten acres of land for five hundred dollars. The parcel overlooked a granite ledge that had snagged dozens of vessels and claimed as many lives.

John McComb, Jr. again received the construction contract. The seventy-three-foot lighthouse, of similar design to his other towers, along with a two-story dwelling and an oil vault banked into a hillside, were all completed in early 1799 under the administration of President John Adams.

The Building Years

The lighthouses at Cape Henry, Montauk Point, and Eatons Neck—among the first sentinels authorized by the new federal government—were the inaugural projects in a flurry of activity to further civilize American shores and establish the new nation in overseas commerce. Profitable routes to the Far East, Russia, and the

The first lighthouse to guide shipping through western Long Island Sound went into service at Eatons Neck in 1799. It stood on land originally purchased from the Matinecock Indians in 1646 by Theophilus Eaton, a London merchant and governor of New Haven, Connecticut. At the time the lighthouse was proposed, the land belonged to the Gardiner family, who sold it to the government for five hundred dollars. Perhaps as a result of the Gardiners' influence in New York politics or their charity in formerly maintaining a pole beacon on Eatons Neck, nineteen-year-old John H. Gardiner was appointed lightkeeper. No description of duties or formal standards had yet been adopted for lighthouse work, but Gardiner was assigned to keep a lookout for ships in distress and was given a boat to assist anyone who needed him. Only two years later he was replaced, since he had spent more time on his farm than at the lighthouse. The new keeper, John Squires, was appointed at a salary of two hundred dollars a year and admonished to live at the station full time.

Lanterns Anchored at Sea

Day after day, day after day,
We struck, nor breath, nor motion;
As idle as a painted ship
Upon a painted ocean.
Samuel Taylor Coleridge,
"The Rime of the Ancient Mariner," 1798

Imagine a fleet of ships with a go-nowhere mission, ships whose sole purpose is to sit anchored in the water, pitching and rolling with the waves as markers of seaway hazards. The lightships—a combination of lighthouse and ship—comprised just such a fleet. By day their colorfully painted hulls contrasted with the sea-green water and blue sky; by night they shone like bright stars afloat on the horizon. In foul weather their bells bonged or horns croaked to warn other ships of their presence.

From 1820 to 1967, these briny traffic signals guided shipping in the Mid-Atlantic. The first lightship in the United States went into service at Willoughby Spit, Virginia, in 1820. It was a small lightboat with a single mast on which a lantern was attached. Its lone lamplighter rowed to it nightly to light the beacon and returned at dawn to extinguish it.

A ship permanently anchored in the water was a curiosity for early-nineteenth-century sailors. Watermen in the Chesapeake tell a yarn about a fisherman who, upon seeing Janes Island Lightship for the first time in the 1820s, thought it had gone aground. He offered to refloat the vessel but was told it was "a lightship." He replied, a bit annoyed, that he could tow a light ship or a heavy one.

Two sizes of lightships came into use. Small vessels displaced one hundred tons or less and were suitable for protected waters; larger lightships, which could go as big as three hundred tons, served in more exposed waters, anchored off the coastline miles at sea. Lightships had little or no motive power at first and included a bulky, flattened hull with a bilge keel added to reduce rolling in heavy seas. Huge, mushroom-shaped anchors dug firmly into the seabed and held the ships on position.

Storms or the movement of ice sometimes dragged the anchor or parted its chain, setting a lightship adrift. Cape Charles Lightship was blown off station three times between 1896 and 1936. A tender towed it back to its assigned position each time, but even there it was at risk. In 1912, a ship rammed it. Such collisions were commonplace, for lightships stood duty in busy sea lanes.

During storms, lightships remained on station at great risk in order to prevent other ships from running onto shoals. The various lightships anchored at Five Fathom Bank, about fifteen miles off Cape May, were among those most exposed to the fury of Atlantic storms. Heavy seas in the winter of 1867 set Five Fathom Bank Lightship No. 18 adrift twice.

She was pushed off station four more times between 1872 and 1881. A hurricane destroyed the lightship on August 24, 1893, when four successive heavy waves hit her broadside. Most of the crew washed overboard. Survivors managed to launch a lifeboat before the vessel sank. It was the first lightship in the nation destroyed while anchored on station.

While the early lightships were tended by only one or two men, who lived ashore and rowed out to the vessel each night, larger lightships with full-time resident crews became the norm after about 1850 and remained so until the 1980s, when lightships went out of service. Tours of duty on each vessel averaged five to seven years during the period of the Lighthouse Board and Bureau of Lighthouses, and two to four years in the Coast Guard era. Crew members often alternated assignments aboard lighthouses and tenders.

As a rule, lightship duty was considered an unpleasant assignment. Sailors of merchant and military ships, as well as the public, regarded a stationary vessel as something less than a ship, yet not as reputable as a lighthouse. A popular yarn told among lightship crewmen in the 1950s concerned a veteran of lightships who was asked to return to duty. His reply: "If it weren't for the disgrace it would bring upon my family, I'd rather go to state prison." In spite of its unsung status, lightship duty was critical to safety at sea and a calling for some. Most, however, did their time and went to sea on other, more respectable ships.

Similar to lighthouse duty on a waterbound tower, lightship work was dangerous on occasion, but more often tedious. Crews of six to twelve men, nicknamed "fish," lived on board in cramped quarters, ate mundane meals of salt beef and biscuits, and did repetitive jobs. There was no change of scenery for long periods. If visibility was poor, the fogbells and horns deprived even the hardiest man of sleep. Seasickness was a problem, too, since lightships rolled constantly. Some men couldn't overcome it and had special lightship duty waivers in their service records.

The deck of a lightship was cluttered with machinery used to maintain the beacon and fog signal, but the hallmark of a lightship—the signature that made it easily identifiable at sea—was the light basket or light cage. Most large lightships had two mounted near the top of masts. The earliest beacons were oil lamps, which were fueled on deck then hauled up the masts on little pulley systems. Gimbals kept the lamps level as the ship rolled in the waves. Later, gas and electric lights with small lenses provided increased brilliance.

Advances in marine engineering eventually rendered lightships obsolete. Lighthouses on screwpile and caissons foundations, large buoys, and Texas towers replaced the small lightship at anchor. The last lightship on duty in the Mid-Atlantic was Chesapeake No. 116, taken out of service in 1980. It's now a museum piece at Baltimore Maritime Museum. Several others have been preserved, including Ambrose Lightship, on display at New York South Street Seaport, and a No. 101 at Portsmouth, Virginia. Barnegat Lightship languishes at Camden Shipyard in Philadelphia, waiting for preservation, and Overfalls Lightship No. 118 is moored at Lewes, Delaware.

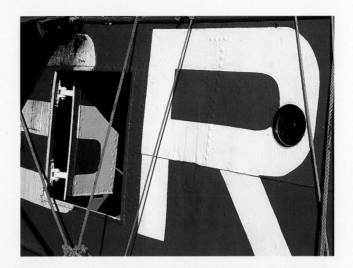

Both photos: Upstaged by a Texas tower–style lighthouse in 1967, Ambrose Lightship was retired to the South Street Seaport Museum in New York City. During its active years, the bright red hull made it easy to spot at sea during the day and huge letters identified its station. By night its two light baskets signaled the final leg into the channel of New York Harbor.

East Indies needed bolstering, and building lighthouses at busy U.S. ports was essential to trade. New England dominated the construction era, building lights at places like Portland Harbor and the Kennebec River, Bakers Island north of Boston, Gay Head on Martha's Vineyard, and the Highlands of Cape Cod. In the South, towers rose at Cape Hatteras and Ocracoke on the Outer Banks of the Carolinas, and the Cape Fear and Savannah Rivers. In all, twelve new lighthouses were constructed under the administration of President George Washington. By the turn of the nineteenth century, that number had doubled.

As the nation grew, government grew, and with that growth came the difficulties of politics and partisanship. Changes in administration would hinder the lighthouse service nearly all of its years. In 1792, Alexander Hamilton created the Office of the Commissioner of Revenue and gave it control of lighthouses, but in 1802, President Thomas Jefferson abolished the office and placed control of the lighthouses back in the hands of the Treasury Department. Eleven years later, the Commissioner of Revenue was reinstated, with lighthouses falling again under its aegis. The reason for the changes may have been little more than growing pains in a new government plagued by debt and unsure of its course, but for the lighthouses it meant a lack of stability and little room for technological growth.

The Mid-Atlantic saw several important lights established before the War of 1812. In the Chesapeake Bay, busy Hampton Roads was lit in 1802 at Old Point Comfort, marking the mouth of the James River, and again in 1804 at New Point Comfort, at the entrance to Mobjack Bay. The opening into the Chesapeake was a mariner's nightmare; riddled with shoals and mudflats, it was coursed by currents from strong tributaries and the bay's opposing tides. Vessels destined for the James River steered for Old Point Comfort Light, while those seeking the York River or points north sought New Point Comfort Light.

In 1805, Little Gull Island at the eastern end of Long Island Sound was marked by a fifty-six-foot stone tower to help ships entering the sound navigate the "Horse Race," a strong tidal swath that could run as swift as five knots. This beacon was joined four years later by Sands Point Light at the western end of Long Island Sound where ships made their way into New York Harbor through the notorious bottleneck known as "Hell's Gate."

Additionally, Congress allotted money to establish pole lights on major navigable rivers, such as the Hudson,

the Delaware, and various large tributaries feeding the Chesapeake Bay. Lamplighters were hired to maintain oil lanterns at river entrances and danger points along their courses. The lamplighters were not paid well, nor was their work checked or regulated; thus, the early river lights were seldom dependable.

More lighthouses and a better system of operating them might have arisen at this time had the War of 1812 not intervened, occupying the government's concerns and emptying the national treasury. Again, lighthouses became pawns. Americans extinguished the beacons to prevent them from aiding the British, while the British attempted to use them to their advantage. Cape Henlopen was extinguished, and all buoys were removed from the Delaware Bay. Old Point Comfort Light at Fort Monroe was darkened by the Americans, then captured by the British and used as a lookout point.

When the war ended, existing lighthouses were repaired and returned to service, but there was no money to build new towers. The lighthouse service languished for a time, while the administration again changed. The Office of the Commissioner of Revenue was abolished for the final time in 1820, and responsibility for lighthouses again was placed in the Treasury Department.

Lean Years and Government Scandal

The planning and construction of lighthouses, fog signals, and buoys at important points along the Eastern Seaboard desperately needed to resume. The man appointed to the mission was Stephen Pleasanton, a parsimonious accountant who served as the first Fifth Auditor in the Treasury Department, an office created by President James Monroe to handle the fiscal business of the developing nation. Pleasanton knew little about lighthouses and the technology surrounding them but had sufficient management experience to earn the position. "He was," according to historian F. Ross Holland, "zealous, hardworking, conservative, and an overly conscientious guardian of the public dollar." Pleasanton's thirty-two-year tenure as overseer of the lighthouse service saw the construction of 270 lighthouses; the establishment of lightships; an increase in the number of buoys, range lights, and fog signals; and the beginnings of a standardized and well-regulated lighthouse system. Unfortunately, Pleasanton is not remembered for these accomplishments; rather, his tenure is known as one of deleterious tight-fistedness and political favoritism.

Unwilling to educate himself about the nature of lighthouse work, for Pleasanton had plenty of other duties to occupy his time in the Treasury Department, he relied on local collectors of customs to supervise lighthouses in their districts while he managed the fiscal end of the business. The collectors were highly influential in decisions regarding the placement, construction, and staffing of lighthouses. Pleasanton took pride in being able to operate below cost and valued the lowest bidder. In an effort to encourage economy and conformity, he decided to consolidate contracts for building light towers, installing illuminating mechanisms, and supplying oil and equipment.

Winslow Lewis, a retired sea captain and contractor from Wellfleet, Massachusetts, in 1812 persuaded the government to adopt his patented illuminating apparatus for all its lighthouses. He was then quick to realize that Pleasanton needed an advisor on matters pertaining to lighthouses. He took advantage of the Fifth Auditor's consolidation plan and secured for himself numerous contracts to build lighthouses, outfit them with his lighting system, and supply oil.

Lewis accomplished what Pleasanton required of him—the construction and outfitting of lighthouses on a shoestring budget. His bids were exceedingly low, and the work he did often reflected this. Many of the towers he built were later condemned for poor workmanship, and he was criticized for steering Pleasanton in an outdated direction and gaining his favor through personal friendship. Consequently, many of the lighthouses built between 1820 and 1850 were of poor construction and operated with antiquated technology. Only a few from this period still stand today.

Among the survivors is Concord Point Light, situated where the mighty Susquehanna River surges into the Chesapeake Bay. The builder, John Donahoo, was a Revolutionary War veteran, commissioner in the town, and friend of Winslow Lewis. In 1822, he built a retaining wall for Bodkin Point Lighthouse on the Patapsco River, and two years later he won the bid for Thomas Point Shoal Lighthouse south of Annapolis. As Donahoo began construction at Concord Point in 1826, the foundation of the tower at Thomas Point was failing. Donahoo knew he had to do a better job this time or face the loss of future contracts.

He built well, giving the thirty-two-foot tower thick, stable granite walls and a hand-hewn stone spiral stairway. Lewis's lighting apparatus topped the structure and sent its light a few miles into the bay. Donahoo went on to build eleven more light towers in the Chesapeake Bay. Local historians call them "Donahoo's Dozen." Most were modest conical masonry structures with iron lanterns and detached keepers' quarters. Lewis's patented lighting system was installed in each lantern.

Under Pleasanton's circumspect hand, the lighthouse service moved into a period of stepped-up construction. The nation's first lightship was anchored at Willoughby Spit, Virginia, in 1820. After a severe winter of exposure to ice and wind, the seventy-ton vessel with its single light basket was moved to Craney Island at Norfolk. Four more lightships were commissioned in 1821 to anchor at various spots in the Chesapeake Bay and in 1823 at Brandywine Shoal, Cross Ledge, and Five Fathom Bank in the Delaware Bay. Also in that year, the nation's first outside lightship—anchored in the open ocean—was stationed off Sandy Hook. Numerous lighthouses were planned and built in these years, too, but little forethought went into the placement and operation of some, and little money as well. The result was an assembly of aids that were a poor reflection of the engineering technology, knowledge, and materials available at the time.

At Cape May, a critical point for vessels entering the Delaware Bay from the north, the Pennsylvania Board of Port Wardens had purchased land for a lighthouse in 1785. Maps and documents of the period show a crude light on the point, but it was 1822 before Congress appropriated money for a lighthouse. An octagonal masonry structure equipped with Lewis's lamp system was illuminated in October 1824 on the dunes of the point. The folly of building here was soon evident. Keeper Ezekial Stevens watched the shoreline erode week by week and sent word that the tower would soon be threatened. By 1837, he was ordered to extinguish the lamps, and construction of a new tower was begun farther back from sea.

Only two years after the lighting of Cape May, funds were designated for a lighthouse at Navesink, overlooking Sandy Hook. It seemed judicious to place a landfall beacon here, since the Highlands were the loftiest spot on the Atlantic Seaboard, providing considerable elevation and range. It was decided that twin lights should be built to distinguish Navesink from the single beacon of nearby Sandy Hook.

The practice of constructing twin light stations was not new in America or elsewhere. England and Scotland had them, and triple lights were in use at the Casquets off northern France. Several sets of twin lights already operated in New England by this time as well. The idea was to differentiate one beacon from another, since nearly all lights at this time were white and fixed.

President Thomas Jefferson appointed the lightkeepers at both Old Point Comfort Light (above), lit in 1802 at Hampton Roads, and the 1804 New Point Comfort Light (right) at the entrance to Mobjack Bay. He was justifiably proud that the towers stood in his home state of Virginia, but he cautioned that lightkeepers should be discharged for the smallest "degrees of remissness, because of the calamities which even these produce."

Work was begun on two octagonal bluestone towers, situated 320 feet apart with a keeper's dwelling between them. The cost for the twin towers, house, and optics ran $10,290. In a surprising turn of events, David Melville of Rhode Island, not Winslow Lewis, supplied the lamps and reflectors for each tower. The structures quickly began to deteriorate, however, and investigation showed they had been poorly built, no doubt as a result of Stephen Pleasanton's penchant for accepting the lowest bid.

The lighthouse service then turned its attention to the Hudson River. The opening of the Erie Canal in 1825 had increased navigation on the Hudson, which served as a portal to the sea via the canal's outlet at Albany. Stony Point Lighthouse was lit in 1826 on the river's western shores in Rockland County. It was joined by three more lighthouses at Roundout, Saugerties, and Esopus Meadows in the 1830s, each marking dangerous curves and rock outcroppings. While Stony Point Light was elevated above the river, its compatriots stood at water's edge and suffered annual damage from ice and flooding. Most eventually were rebuilt.

On the Atlantic Seaboard, lighthouses were built on the barrier beaches of Fire Island in 1826 and Barnegat Inlet in 1835. Trypots for the whaling industry had long burned on Fire Island, bestowing its name, but ships needed a greater light to guide them from Montauk Point past the sandbars of Long Island's south shore into New York Bay. The octagonal, eighty-four-foot Fire Island Light was outfitted with Winslow Lewis's lighting system, but neither its height nor its beacon were adequate. Ships often went aground looking for it. While the Pleasanton administration pondered what to do, money went to other projects. At Barnegat Inlet, New Jersey's most hazardous ingress, Lewis won the contract to build a seacoast light. Since Lewis enjoyed considerable autonomy in the design of lighthouses, he built nothing more than a harbor beacon, far too small and feeble to deter shipwreck along this busy part of the coast. One sea captain claimed he could not distinguish Barnegat Inlet Light from a ship's lantern.

System Overhaul

Self-examination and change were on the horizon for the lighthouse service. Mariners complained bitterly that U.S. lights were inferior to those of Europe and inadequately maintained. Many structures were crumbling. Lights were sometimes inactive for long periods, or their characteristics changed without notification so ships were misled. Lightkeepers received no training as to the operation and care of the illuminating mechanisms, and they repeatedly groused about the poor quality of oil, cheap workmanship of the lamps, and low pay. Many keepers were considered of low character. In 1827, naval officer William B. Barney remarked that the keeper at North Port Lighthouse in the Chesapeake Bay had "become a disgrace to any keeper . . . [and] appears perfectly indifferent to his duty."

At Sandy Hook Lighthouse, another naval officer noted that the lamp wicks were not trimmed during the night, as per instructions, because "in the keeper's opinion, they do not require it." Nor did the keeper follow other directives to maintain a journal, weather records, and a list of expenditures and oil consumption. In all matters, it seemed "the keeper uses his own discretion."

In 1837, Stephen Pleasanton requested a large sum of money to improve the system and build thirty-one new lighthouses, but before funding was approved Congress demanded an investigation to determine how it should be spent. The Navy sent twenty-two officers to visit lighthouses in all the U.S. lighthouse districts, which by now included the Gulf of Mexico, the Great Lakes, and many inland waterways. The following year, the Eastern Seaboard was divided into six districts. A naval officer was assigned to superintend each district and was given his own revenue cutter for the purpose of inspections.

Additionally, two French-made prism lenses were purchased for testing in the Navesink Twin Lights. Called Fresnel lenses, for the French physicist who devised them, they arrived in 1840 wearing a hefty price tag of $18,975—some ten times the cost for the Lewis lenses. They proved far superior in clarity, brilliance, and dependability, utilizing 90 percent of the light from lamps and requiring only half the oil. But penurious Pleasanton decided not to purchase more Fresnel lenses, deeming them too expensive.

The Navy returned its report to Congress regarding the condition of America's lighthouses. The conclusions of the twenty-two individual investigating officers were

One of "Donahoo's Dozen," Concord Point Lighthouse was the second of twelve sentinels built by Revolutionary War veteran John Donahoo, whose construction work was well known in the Chesapeake Bay area in the early years of the nineteenth century. Concord Point is one of only five lighthouses in the nation with a hand-hewn granite spiral stairway.

Facing page: In 1623, Cornelius Jacob Mey of Holland's West India Company sailed into the Delaware Bay and named the northern point of land at its mouth in honor of himself. Mey's conceited christening was later changed to "May" by mapmakers. The point's graceful 157-foot lighthouse, with a distinctive red lantern, replaced two earlier light towers, one destroyed by erosion in 1847 and the other by weather in 1859. Its benevolent beam has seen its share of tragedy, including a suicide leap from the lantern gallery in the late 1990s.

Left: Eight multiple-light stations were built in the United States in the nineteenth century, but only one set stood in the mid-Atlantic region. Navesink Twin Lights were established in 1828 to eliminate confusion for the mariner, who was greeted by a number of white, fixed lights congregated along the shipping corridor leading into New York Harbor. Two lights on the Highlands at Navesink helped distinguish it from nearby single beacons. Rebuilt and re-lit in 1862, the station resembles a fort.

starkly similar. The United States lagged behind in technology, and its navigational aids were badly managed. Lightkeepers were hired without consideration of skill, poorly paid, and seldom made accountable for their work. Many of the lighthouses in operation were in shameful condition. Foundations and mortar were giving out, glass in the lanterns was inferior and caused distortion of light, reflectors were worn out, wooden parts had rotted, and towers leaked. Some had been poorly situated and were of little service to the mariner; in other locations there was overlighting.

It seemed the incumbent administration had not consulted with those who most needed and used lighthouses—naval and civilian shipmasters—to determine where the lights should be built and what character they should exhibit. A uniform system of buoys, lights, and colorful daymarks to identify the towers during daylight hours was suggested, plus an all-out investment in up-to-date optics and an adequately trained, regulated crew of lightkeepers. While Congress admitted Pleasanton had worked miracles with little money, his effort was criticized as being far too single-mindedly frugal at the expense of safety at sea.

Additional investigations and reports were made in the early 1840s, including one by a congressional committee on commerce and another by I. W. P. Lewis, the estranged nephew of Winslow Lewis. Both were condemnatory, and the younger Lewis's report hinted strongly at political misconduct. Pleasanton took a defensive posture and produced piles of paperwork and affidavits from shipmasters to justify his actions over the previous two decades. Congress reacted by sending two respected naval officers abroad to inspect the lighthouses of Europe and make a comparison to the U.S. system. Their report in 1846 recommended a total reorganization of the U.S. lighthouse service.

In the face of such incriminating evidence, Congress idled. Five years dragged by while a committee considered what to do. Finally, in March 1851, Maryland congressman Alexander Evans proposed that "hereafter . . . the lens and Fresnel system shall be adopted," resulting in passage of an act that authorized the secretary of the treasury to purchase and install Fresnel lenses in major U.S. coastal lighthouses as promptly as possible. Congress also appointed a board of military officers, scientists, and engineers for yet another investigation. The resulting 762-page report confirmed earlier grievances:

Bombay Hook Light—Duncan Stewart, keeper—89 years old; daughters keep light . . . no plastering of tower. . . .

Navesink Lights—James D. Hubbard, principal keeper. No vocation; was a farmer when made keeper. . . . Dwelling leaks; stable and shop out of order . . . no proper means for warming the oil . . . no system of supplies. . . .

Sandy Hook Light-House—David J. Patterson, principal and only keeper; hires an assistant out of his own pay. . . .

Bodkin Point Light-House—William H. Glover, keeper . . . has no measurer to measure the oil; guesses at the quantity of oil used . . . has no means of ascertaining the hour of the night . . . oil last year very bad. . . .

Cape May Lighthouse—Tower rough and rudely built, leaking, unpainted, rusty. . . . Keeper untrained. He had no printed instructions and is in a low state of morale.

A year later, the U.S. Lighthouse Establishment was abolished and replaced by the nine-member U.S. Lighthouse Board. Over the next half-century, this new administration would create a system of aids to navigation unequalled anywhere in the world.

Above and facing page: With the opening of the Erie Canal in 1825, traffic on the Hudson River increased. To meet the stepped-up demands of navigation, four lighthouses were soon built on the route to Albany. Saugerties Lighthouse opened in 1836 to mark the mouth of Esopus Creek but was destroyed by a flood twenty years later. It was replaced by a stone house and lantern on a pier in 1869 (facing page). Esopus Meadows Light (above) came into service in 1839 to mark a series of dangerous mudflats in the river north of Poughkeepsie. Also destroyed by a flood, it was replaced in 1871 with a quaint cottage-style sentinel nicknamed "Maid of the Meadows." Automated since 1965, the little landmark has suffered from vandalism. The Save the Esopus Meadows Lighthouse Commission has painted curtains on its windows to fool would-be trespassers into thinking it still is occupied.

DAYMARKS

*Nothing that has to do with the appearance of a light tower is by happenstance,
but by carefully planned design and all for the purposes of easy identification.*
Hans Christian Adamson, *Keepers of the Lights*, 1955

Lighthouses wear beautiful dresses—or so we think!
Those colorful gowns of paint may enhance their
nautical ambience, but the true intent is to help
mariners identify light towers by day. A variety of patterns in
bright colors, stripes, spirals, and fanciful checkers differentiate one lighthouse from another. These bold designs show
up easily against a confusing backdrop of buildings or stand
out from the natural landscape.

Assateague Light's candy-stripe daymark stands out well
against the Virginia pines surrounding it. The new Cape
Henry Light wears alternating faces of black and white to
separate it from tawny sands. Red bands on the towers at
neighboring Barnegat Inlet and Absecon clearly indicate
who's who by their unique arrangement. Colors also might
indicate channel directions, as in the bright red of Jeffries
Hook Light, which marks the right side of the Hudson River
channel.

The shape and height of a lighthouse also serve to identify it. Horton Point's square white tower, for example, is
easily distinguished from its neighbors on the north shore
of Long Island. The twin towers of Navesink are unmistak-
ably castle-like and elevated high above the surrounding
New Jersey shoreline. Cottage-style sentinels, such as those
at Point Lookout, Maryland, and East Point and Hereford,
New Jersey, imitate houses with small lanterns rising from
their roofs. The tiered towers at Orient Point and Romer
Shoal, New York, have earned the descriptive sobriquet
"sparkplug" for their uncanny resemblance to the same.
Whether conical, octagonal, cylindrical, square, housetop,
skeleton, or some other form—each presents a distinct out-
line.

Descriptions of daymarks are an important part of light
lists, the catalogs mariners use to determine the location
and character of lighthouses. Daymarks change as the needs
of shipping change or when lighthouses are added or removed. Having an up-to-date guidebook is vital, so the Coast
Guard publishes an annual *Light List* and sends out "No-
tices to Mariners" about changes during the year. Details
for each lighthouse clearly distinguish it from its luminous
brethren. In the 1994 edition, for example, Smith Point
Lighthouse at the entrance to the Potomac River was listed
as a "white brick square tower and octagonal dwelling on
brown cylindrical pier."

Old light lists reveal how daymarks evolve. *Lighthouses
of the World*, published in 1877 in London, described the
original Cape Henry Light as a "white tower near sand hills."
Today, with no beacon in its lantern, it truly is only a
daymark, but a mottled brown one instead of white. H. P.

*Sharps Island Lighthouse near Tilghman Island in Chesa-
peake Bay created it own daymark in the 1970s when ice
and erosion damage caused it to lean. An expensive stabili-
zation plan is under consideration, but ultimately, the tower
may have to be abandoned and demolished by the Coast
Guard.*

Imray's 1931 edition of *Lights and Tides of the World* listed
Assateague Lighthouse as a "conical red tower." Its current
daymark is red and white stripes. Montauk Point Light did
not always wear its broad band of brown nor did Fire Island
always have stripes. Early on, these were white towers, but
by 1903 the addition of other lights along the seaboard necessitated more singular daymarks.

One of the oddest daymarks is that of Sharps Island Light
in the Chesapeake Bay, originally painted dark purple. Its
plum garb is now faded brown, and it has gained notoriety
in the *Light List* for having its own personal "list." Ice floes
in the 1970s caused it to lean fifteen degrees. Canted and
sun-bleached, it can truly be said to be "out of plumb."

Above: *In the 1800s, daymarks grew more elaborate and colorful, evidenced by the candy-stripe paint scheme of Assateague Light at Chincoteague, Virginia. Its winsome dress is designed to help it show up distinctly against the trees and tidal marshes surrounding it.*

Above, right: *A number of charming little screwpile lighthouses, like this one that once stood at Drum Point, were scattered throughout the Chesapeake Bay. Everything about a lighthouse helps define its appearance for the mariner during the day. A particular aspect of the construction, such as roof color or arrangement of flagpoles, could be an identifying feature.*

Right: *During its early years, New Jersey's Sea Girt Light was one of the few structures on its beach. By the 1940s, it had many neighbors. A Coast Guard Light List description noted it as a brick house surmounted by a square tower and black lantern. Even with these details at hand, it was a challenge for seamen to distinguish the lighthouse from the homes that had sprung up around it.*

CHAPTER 3

Reconstruction & the Rise of Technology

Left: *Screwpile lighthouses, such as this one at Thomas Point in the Chesapeake Bay, are named for their sturdy iron legs. Each leg has a giant flanged foot anchored deep in the muck. The keeper's quarters and light tower perch on top. Of the more than thirty screwpile lighthouses built in the Chesapeake Bay over the years, only Thomas Point Shoal Light continues to operate on its original site.*

Above: *Brandywine Shoal Light, built in 1850 in the Delaware Bay, was the nation's first successful screwpile lighthouse. It stood until 1914 when it was replaced by this caisson-style lighthouse. The iron caisson was fabricated ashore, towed to the site, sunk, and filled with stone or concrete. The sturdy house on top completed the design.*

*Nothing marks more distinctly the stage of civilization
to which any nation has attained than the character
of the aids to safety which it furnishes the mariner
in approaching and leaving its shores.*
An 1874 report of the U.S. Lighthouse Board

On March 4, 1851, President Millard Filmore signed a bill removing control of lighthouses from the office of Stephen Pleasanton and setting up a temporary board to oversee the service. The board was led by Pleasanton's reliable third district inspector, George Mifflin Bache. A year later, the official U.S. Lighthouse Board was launched; it was composed of three Navy officers, three Army officers, and three civilians, including two scientists and the secretary of the treasury.

The U.S. Lighthouse Board went to work immediately, dividing the nation's coastline into eight districts, including a new one on the West Coast, and assigning a Navy officer and Army officer to each district to serve as chief inspector and engineer. Depots were established within each district to maintain and provision lighthouses and lightships, and look after fog signals and buoys. In 1867, the Board set up a general depot on Staten Island to serve as a clearinghouse for supplies and materials and to test new technology. As the service grew, the Board added smaller depots in places such as Lewes, Christiana, Edgemoor, Baltimore, and Portsmouth, and established a schedule of work to improve the system. The Staten Island depot served the Third District, a region from New York to Delaware. Chesapeake Bay and Virginia came under the Fourth District depot at Portsmouth.

At long last, lightkeepers were chosen more carefully and given training before assuming their duties. Larger stations were assigned multiple keepers and each was issued a 152-page handbook called *Instructions to Lightkeepers*. It detailed all operations of the lights and fog signals and established a standard routine for work. Pay improved, as did pride and professionalism. The job took on a quasi-military tenor, heightened by the introduction of uniforms, rank, regular inspections, and awards. In addition, the board began keeping personnel records and requiring logbooks to be kept at each station.

A massive new construction and rebuilding effort was launched to add needed beacons and replace deteriorating towers, as well as upgrade equipment. Before the Civil War, towers at Fire Island, Mispillion River, Barnegat Inlet, and Cape May were rebuilt, and the Lewis reflector system was rendered all but obsolete,

Above: *In the 1870s, the U.S. Lighthouse Board maintained discipline and fostered esprit de corps by instituting ranks and prescribing uniforms for lighthouse service personnel. The handsome blue wool jacket of lighthouse keepers had brass buttons decorated with small lighthouses and rank insignia on the lapels. The hardboard cap bore the service emblem. National Park Service historian Tom Hoffman dons the period uniform to give today's visitors a feel for the past at Sandy Hook Light.*

Facing page: *Many of the lighthouses built prior to the era of the U.S. Lighthouse Board were of poor quality. Fire Island Lighthouse on the south shore of Long Island was among those rebuilt in the 1850s. Taller than its predecessor, it was painted in a yellow daymark that quickly earned it the nickname "The Winking Woman," for its comely shape and bright color. The daymark was changed to black and white in 1891.*

replaced by new Fresnel lenses. Scientific study and experimentation in lighthouse science, or pharology, was begun. Cheaper and more plentiful fuels, such as colza and lard oil, supplanted expensive whale oil. New and better lightships were commissioned, buoys and fog signaling improved, and up-to-date construction technologies were implemented.

Lights on Legs and Lights of Iron

Among the novel engineering designs was the screwpile lighthouse. This spider-legged tower, developed in England in the 1830s, proved suitable for unstable submarine foundations such as mucky estuaries and bays. It could be fabricated on shore and snapped together on site with relative ease; it also was lighter in weight and less costly than a masonry tower. The first screwpile lighthouse built in the United States went into service on Brandywine Shoal in the Delaware Bay. It replaced the problematic lightship anchored there—a vessel battered by ice in winter and which frequently broke its moorings.

Construction of the Brandywine Shoal screwpile beacon began in 1848, directed by Major Hartman Bache of the U.S. Department of Topographical Engineers. He opted for a round, cast-iron plate tower supported by nine iron pilings. The entire structure stood in six feet of water and was heavily braced by an ice fender. Its third-order fixed Fresnel lens, purchased in Paris, outshone all other lights in the bay, and a five-hundred-pound fogbell sent melodious tones over the water. Bache reported that the interior provided a comfortable dwelling for the lightkeepers: "The first floor is divided into kitchen, store-room, and hall, with stairway leading to the second floor, which is divided into two sleeping areas."

Though the Delaware Bay was the site of the first screwpile light in America, it was the Chesapeake Bay, with its many shallow hazards, where the design found a welcome home. More than forty screwpile lighthouses were built here, beginning with the Puncoteague River Light in 1854. Unfortunately, this small beacon was not adequately braced and ice carried it away. Its successors were made sturdier and protected by a circular wall of riprap. Ice remained the major threat in the bay and claimed a number of other screwpile lighthouses. The most notable was Sharps Island Lighthouse, ripped off its iron legs by an ice floe in February 1881 and carried five miles down the bay from its assigned perch at the mouth of the Choptank River. Its two terrified attendants

Invented by a blind Irish engineer in 1831, the screwpile revolutionized lighthouse construction by enabling builders to anchor foundations into a soft, alluvial seabed. More than forty screwpile lighthouses were built in the Delaware and Chesapeake Bays in the nineteenth century, but only four are still in existence, including deactivated Hooper Strait Lighthouse now on exhibit at Chesapeake Bay Maritime Museum in St. Michaels, Maryland. A screw from one of its foundation pilings is also displayed at the museum.

rode out the ordeal until the lighthouse grounded, then dutifully salvaged the lens, tools, and any furniture they could haul ashore.

As foundries produced more cast iron, lighthouse engineers increasingly chose it as a material for lanterns, galleries, stairways, and even the towers themselves. The screwpile lighthouse built in 1855 in the shallows of Seven Foot Knoll, where the Patapsco River entered Chesapeake Bay, was the ultimate metallic sentinel; its iron-pile legs supported an iron-plate, cottage-style house from which rose an iron gallery and lantern. All parts for the lighthouse were fabricated in Baltimore, then shipped out to the site and assembled piece by piece in about three months time. This lighthouse was not only quick and cheap to build, but also more durable and better positioned than the ineffective lighthouse on Bodkin Island it replaced.

In 1883, a cast-iron lighthouse was built for training and testing at the Staten Island depot. This lighthouse would later be moved to Romer Shoal in New York Bay for active duty.

Wooden stairways and lanterns at many old towers were replaced with more durable cast iron following the Civil War. The material also proved sturdier than wood for the pile foundations of screwpile lighthouses. Seven Foot Knoll Lighthouse was built entirely of cast iron in 1855, with many of its parts fabricated in the nearby city of Baltimore by Murray & Hazelhurst. The lighthouse served at the entrance to the Patapsco River for more than century before being moved to Baltimore's Inner Harbor in 1988 and exhibited as a museum piece.

Iron stairways began to upstage wood, providing strength and resistance to wear. Their lightweight, open-framework design brought additional light and ventilation into towers. Wooden lanterns and decks also gave way to iron, reducing the danger of fire. Cape Henlopen Lighthouse was given a new iron lantern in 1854, and its wooden stairs were replaced by a new iron stairway in 1867. Sandy Hook Light received a complete overhaul of its interior in 1857, with the addition of an iron staircase and decks, and an iron lantern. In 1860, iron stairs replaced the wooden stairway at Montauk Point

Light. Similar renovations were made at all older lighthouses on the Eastern Seaboard.

Victorian tastes appeared in the handsome details of tower ironwork. Decorative railing finials and posts—some in the shape of miniature lighthouses—distinctive portholes and fanlights, fancy brackets and stair treads, and elegant doorways were typical embellishments.

Prisoners of War

Amid the flurry of improvements and modernization begun by the U.S. Lighthouse Board, the nation again

Whereas colonial builders strove for economy and simplicity, architects of the Victorian era sometimes added costly details to lighthouses. Renewal of the ironwork on old Montauk Point Light (right) in the 1880s imparted a delicate beauty to its lantern deck. Elegant brackets accentuate the lantern of Staten Island Light (left) in New York.

went to war, this time on its own soil. Lighthouses in New York, New Jersey, and Delaware escaped the turmoil, but many in Maryland and Virginia became blameless victims in the struggle between the Union and Confederacy. Problems arose when the Confederacy claimed sovereignty over lighthouses and other federal buildings within its borders, asserting that these were important to the South's economy and needed to be maintained under local, not federal, control. Southern lightkeepers, collectors of customs, and other U.S. Lighthouse Board personnel were informed that they would work for the Confederacy or relinquish their jobs.

On March 6, 1861, the Confederate States Lighthouse Bureau was created by Jefferson Davis, President of the Confederacy, whose love for lighthouses traced back to his Congressional work in the 1840s, when he procured funds for lighthouse construction at important spots along the Gulf of Mexico. The new Confederate effort was similar to the U.S. Lighthouse Board. Confederate States Navy Commander Raphael Semmes of Alabama was placed in charge; he immediately divided the South's lighthouses into four districts and assigned a naval officer to oversee each. Semmes and his cadre had hardly begun their duties when Fort Sumter was fired upon and the war began. Plans for a Confederate reorganization of lighthouses began to fall apart as the South's naval officers were called to duty at sea.

Virginia seceded from the Union in April 1861, and Cape Henry Lighthouse was attacked within days by Southern vandals who considered the tower a Union aid.

Assistant Keeper John B. Drew reported that men from Princess Anne County entered the station willfully and destroyed its illuminating apparatus. The lighthouse was guarded for the remainder of the war, and it was repaired and back in operation early in 1863. Other lighthouses at Southern ports were extinguished so that they could not aid the Union blockaders. In most cases, the lenses and all equipment were seized and hidden safely away or buried in the sand, while the towers were left dark and empty. In the lower Chesapeake Bay, all lightships were ruined or sunk by the Confederates, who intended to relight them as soon as Union forces retreated and a victory was assured.

In the James River, the Union dismantled a number of screwpile lighthouses in 1862 to keep them from being destroyed or aiding the rebellion. Most were reinstated in 1864 after the river became a major artery for transporting Union supplies. The Lighthouse Board relighted them dubiously, noting, "Their permanency will depend upon their protection from the enemy." Gunboats were stationed throughout the region to protect them.

For lightkeepers in Virginia and Maryland, the war was a time of peril. Some were accused of aiding the Confederacy, while others feared for their jobs and safety. R. J. Marshall, keeper of Maryland's Piney Point Lighthouse in 1863, was forced to shut down the general store and grocery he operated as a side business, since he was suspected of selling supplies and food to both the Blue and the Gray. Jean M. Potts, keeper at Hog Island Light in Virginia, sent a worried letter to the Lighthouse Board in September 1863: "I begin to feel alarmed about my own safety, since I voted for the Union candidate. . . . I was the only man who voted the Union Ticket in this precinct." Only a month before, Rebels destroyed the nearby lighthouse on Smith Island and robbed the keeper, who fled. Potts enlisted the help of neighbors to protect his lighthouse and felt secure when a Union ship

Located near a federal prisoner of war camp, Point Lookout Lighthouse seemed a beacon of despair for thousands of Confederate detainees during the Civil War. Today it wears a kinder countenance as the showpiece in a Maryland state park.

Facing page and above: The Civil War was a time of fear and uncertainly at many mid-Atlantic lighthouses. The keeper of Piney Point Lighthouse (facing page) in Maryland was accused of selling goods to the enemy and was forced to shut down a store he operated as a side business. On the Eastern Shore, the lightkeeper at lonely Hog Island Lighthouse (above) lost much of his personal property to "ruffian" sailors from a Union ship anchored off the station to protect the light. (Historical photograph courtesy of the United States Coast Guard)

anchored offshore. However, the "ruffians" aboard soon emptied Potts's garden, chicken house, and smokehouse and helped themselves to his tools and furniture.

At Old Point Comfort Light, the keeper watched in horror in March 1862 as the ironclad Confederate ship *Virginia* attacked and sank the Union frigates *Cumberland* and *Congress*. Moving up the Chesapeake Bay, Confederate forces sacked Back River Lighthouse. At Blackstone Lighthouse, Rebel soldiers destroyed the lens and lamp and took the oil. When keeper Jerome McWilliams saw that they intended to dynamite the tower, he pleaded with them to spare the station, saying his wife was pregnant. Mrs. McWilliams's delicate condition was noted, and the men left. The station was protected by a Union gunboat for the remainder of the war.

At Point Lookout Lighthouse, Keeper Pamelia Edwards kept an anxious vigil over the beacon, which was located only a short distance from a federal prisoner of war camp. Funeral details frequently passed by the lighthouse; more than four thousand Confederate soldiers died in the prison and were buried on the grounds. Even today their presence is felt in eerie reports of ghosts around the sentinel. Edwards was rumored to have kept prisoners in the lighthouse itself, but this is unlikely, considering that the staff of the nearby Union hospital accused her of being a Rebel sympathizer.

When the Civil War ended, many lighthouses stood in ruins, but the Lighthouse Board was fortunate to have the cooperation of communities in Maryland and Virginia. Towers and keepers' quarters were repaired. Lenses were dug out of the sand, cleaned, and reinstalled. Tools were returned, keepers were reinstated, and normal operations resumed.

Improvements in Illumination and Engineering

Following the war, the Lighthouse Board accelerated its development of newer and better illuminants and methods of construction.

By this time, Fresnel lenses of various orders, or sizes, had replaced outdated optics in all but a few minor lights, and new fuels burned in these modernized lamps. Mineral oil, also called kerosene, was tested in a special building at the Staten Island depot in the 1870s, and new lamps were designed to handle the volatile fuel. Concerned about mineral oil's incendiary nature, the Lighthouse Board ordered the construction of detached brick oilhouses to store the fuel. It also issued a serious set of instructions to lightkeepers regarding the handling and storage of mineral oil. Considering that a first-order lens used some 2,300 gallons of fuel annually, the care, use, and accounting of it occupied much of the keeper's time. The first large station to use mineral oil was Navesink Twin Lights in 1883. The new illuminant increased intensity of the beacon in the north tower by two thousand candlepower. The south tower was changed to mineral oil the following year. All major lighthouses were converted to kerosene by 1890.

Incandescent oil vapor lamps, or IOVs, began replacing traditional mineral oil lamps toward the end of the nineteenth century. These used vaporized kerosene and mantles to produce a clean, clear, highly economical light. Owing to the incendiary nature of IOVs,

Jewels of Light

As the evening darkens, lo! How bright,
Through the deep purple of the twilight air,
Beams forth the sudden radiance of its light
With strange, unearthly splendor in its glare.
Henry Wadsworth Longfellow, "The Lighthouse," 1849

The heart of a lighthouse, indeed its very essence, is the great beacon shining in its lantern. How is such brilliance produced? Over the centuries, an assortment of reflecting and magnifying devices evolved, but none so elegantly efficient and beautiful as the Fresnel lens. This opulent gem of prisms and brass transformed the feeble light of oil lamps into piercing rays visible miles at sea, ushering in a new era of illumination in the 1820s. Its invention was at once magical and practical, and the inventor a young man whose acumen was far advanced for his time.

The genius was physicist Augustin-Jean Fresnel (pronounced fray-nel), who had been asked by the French Lighthouse Authority in 1822 to create a better lighthouse beacon. France had ample need for such improvement, since its coast was perilously underlighted. Lighthouses stood on every major island, rock, and headland, but their rays were too weak to be seen beyond the hazards they were intended to mark. Fresnel went to work on a lenticular scheme to harness and concentrate light, intensify it, and then direct it seaward in a powerful beam.

Reflection, refraction, and magnification were at the core of Fresnel's work. He realized that much of the light generated by a lamp was scattered, lost to the mariner. If it could be gathered and focused, the resulting sharp beam would outshine everything around it. Abandoning multiple lamps, he placed a single lamp at the center of a beehive-shaped lens. Concentric rings of prisms, angled to bend light toward the focal plane, worked in concert with a central panel of magnifying glass.

Fresnel devised flashing and fixed lenses in six orders, or sizes. First-order lenses were the largest and most powerful for use as landfall beacons, while sixth-order lenses were the smallest and best suited for small harbors and inlets. Flashing lights employed a series of bull's-eyes of concentric prisms encircling the center of the lens, each one producing a flash. Fixed lights featured a smooth drum of magnifying glass at the center of the lens. Lights were made to revolve by means of a clockworks system with weights suspended in the tower. Keepers wound the weights every few hours, and as the weights fell the lens turned on its pedestal. Early models turned on brass chariot wheels or bearings. Later, heavier lenses rested in troughs of mercury, where high density supported the massive apparatus and low friction allowed it turn almost effortlessly.

An unusual three-and-a-half-order clamshell Fresnel lens is displayed at Montauk Point Lighthouse on Long Island. An aggregate of prisms and brass weighing more than a ton, it required hours to polish. About thirty classical lenses similar to this one still operate in mid-Atlantic lighthouses. Most have retired to museums.

The first lighthouse to receive the new Fresnel technology was the enormous ornate tower at Cordouan, France, where the Gironde River flows into the Bay of Biscay. Seamen from around the world applauded its superior brilliance. The major maritime nations adopted the system immediately, and companies in France and England began manufacturing the lenses. However, the United States considered Fresnel lenses too costly and difficult to install and continued using outdated lighting systems for nearly three decades. By 1850, American lighthouses had fallen far behind those of Europe in brilliance and reliability. With the reorganization of the lighthouse service in 1851, Fresnel lenses were purchased and installed at most major lighthouses.

Over the years, these classic lenses have adapted to changing illuminants, from oil to gas to electricity, even solar power. Some still operate in lighthouses around the nation, but as the Coast Guard has modernized the towers most Fresnel lenses have been given to museums. They are a tribute to a man who died only five years after creating his *magnum opus*, a sculpture of crystal and brass that, though utilitarian, could easily pass for a ballroom chandelier.

Shimmering like a ballroom chandelier, the opulent antique fourth-order lens of Cove Point Lighthouse still operates. The original lens installed in 1857 was illuminated by oil lamps. An incandescent oil vapor apparatus updated it in 1914. When electricity came to the station in 1928, a new French lens was purchased. The final update came in 1986 when the lighting apparatus was automated.

lightkeepers were given careful instructions on their care and operation. Acetylene gas lamps, which came into use around the turn of the nineteenth century, introduced automatic flashers. Tanks of gas were connected to a bellows of sorts that sent bursts of gas to a pilot light. A diaphragm controlled the frequency of bursts to produce flashes of different duration. The addition of a sun relay switch allowed the light to be automated and won the Nobel Prize for its Swedish inventor, Gustav Dahlen.

By 1900, an experimental electric lighthouse had been built at Hell's Gate in eastern Long Island Sound at a cost of eleven thousand dollars. Its fifty-four thousand candlepower electric lights blinded ships and created shadows that were mistaken for reefs. Unsuitable for short-range harbor work, it was abandoned after only two years. But the Statue of Liberty's powerful electric lamps, 305-feet up in her torch and switched on in 1886, worked well, showing twenty-four miles at sea. She was operated as an official lighthouse until 1902.

Electricity made its debut in seacoast stations in 1898 when a seven-ton electric arc lamp and bivalve lens were installed at Navesink Twin Lights. Manufactured in France, the lamp produced a 25-million-candlepower beam, making Navesink the most powerful light station in the United States. The beacon itself was visible twenty-two miles offshore, but sailors claimed its loom could be seen from much farther out and at times reflected off cloud banks up to seventy miles at sea. Not everyone was pleased, however. Dark panels had to be installed on the landward side of the lens to assuage the sleepless residents behind the lighthouse. It would be several decades, however, before electricity reached all lighthouses on the Eastern Seaboard.

Marine engineering was advancing, too, particularly at hazardous offshore sites where ice and heavy seas were problematic. The first caisson lighthouse in the nation was constructed at Craighill Channel Upper Range Light at the entrance to Baltimore Harbor. Here a thick layer of mud lay on the bay floor, suitable only for pile legs. Engineers knew a screwpile structure alone could not stand up to moving ice, so they designed a pile foundation and placed a caisson above it. Piles were driven twenty-seven feet into the muck, leveled, and topped by an iron-plated circular caisson that was filled with concrete. Workers surrounded the submerged base with five thousand tons of stone for stability and mounted a temporary beacon on the caisson. An iron house with a light tower rising from its roof was finished in 1875. The rear light, located 2.4 miles north, was an open-framework tower built on granite piers. It worked in tandem with the front light to provide a range for vessels navigating the tricky channel.

The eastern end of the "Horse Race," a deadly five-knot current coursing Long Island Sound, was marked in 1879 with a caisson beacon off Fishers Island, New York. Considered one of the monumental feats of lighthouse engineering, its story was chronicled twenty years later by its builder, F. Hopkinson Smith, in the true-to-life novel *Caleb West, Master Diver*. Smith's unprecedented and risky plan called for the creation of an artificial island of stone and concrete on the submarine ledge known as Race Rock. On top of this island he built a stone caisson and a granite lighthouse. The project took six years to complete, claimed the lives of two workmen, and cost thirty-four times what was budgeted. Smith was celebrated worldwide for his achievement.

In 1885, a more exposed caisson lighthouse was built at Fourteen Foot Bank in the center of the Delaware Bay. A permanent structure deeply anchored into the bay floor, it was stalwart enough to resist pummeling ice and collisions by ships. It replaced a lightship that had stood watch since the 1820s to mark the Joe Flogger Shoal, which extends into the main shipping channel and is annually tormented by heavy winter ice floes. Hardly a year passed without the lightship being pushed off station, becoming a hazard herself as she drifted aimlessly in the bay.

The Fourteen Foot Bank lighthouse was built using a different technique than was used on other caisson lighthouses. Captain John C. Malley, engineer for the Fourth Lighthouse District, oversaw the project, which was considered highly experimental. Malley's report to the Lighthouse Board in 1886 detailed the work:

On July 5, 1885, the wooden caisson with three tiers of the iron cylinder built upon it, was towed from the Government pier near Lewes, De., to the site and sunk into position by letting water into it. The

Much like the Greek Colossus of Rhodes, Lady Liberty served as a lighthouse when first illuminated. The November 20, 1886, Notice to Mariners carried the news: "The Statue of Liberty Enlightening the World, located on Bedloe's Island, in the harbor of New York, having been placed under the care and superintendence of the Light-House Board, will hereafter be maintained as a beacon; and notice is hereby given that it will be lighted on Monday, the 22d of November, 1886." The powerful electric light in her torch was the first of its kind in a United States lighthouse.

Above: *Because of its twin towers, the station at Navesink, New Jersey was considered an excellent testing site for new technology in illumination. It exhibited the first Fresnel lenses in the United States in the 1840s and was the first station to use mineral oil in 1883. It was also the first seacoast lighthouse to be powered by electricity.*

Right: *The new Cape Henry Lighthouse can be seen through the paned windows of its eighteenth-century predecessor. An 1872 inspection of the old Cape Henry tower revealed cracks running up its walls. Fearing it would collapse, engineers suggested it be retired. The new Cape Henry Lighthouse, a handsome, cast-iron plate tower 157 feet tall, was illuminated in 1882 some 350 feet east of the elder sentinel. The weight of the ironwork was a startling 8,500 tons. Beauty outshone function in its elaborate appointments. The foyer floor was dressed in ornate mosaic tile surrounded by elegant colonnades and wall recesses for oil storage. The unique daymark of alternating black and white panels distinguished it from neighboring lights.*

Two sets of large range lights were built in Craighill Channel in 1873 and 1886 to guide ships into busy Baltimore Harbor. Pictured here is the lower rear range light. A boxy keeper's house that surrounded the base stair cylinder of the tower was demolished following automation.

The nation's first exposed caisson lighthouse was built on Fourteen Foot Bank in the Delaware Bay. The site takes its name from the fact that only fourteen feet of water covers the shoal where the lighthouse is anchored. Surprisingly, many lightkeepers who served at offshore stations like this one couldn't swim. Ed Warrington was returning to Fourteen Foot Bank Light in the 1950s when he fell overboard from the launch. His assistant managed to get a rope around Warrington's arm and saved him from drowning.

Caisson lighthouses solved many of the technical problems of building on offshore sites. Their tiered forms drew curious nicknames, however. Seamen called them "telescoping lighthouses." Those painted white were dubbed "Wedding Cakes." After the advent of automobiles and their familiar spark-producing parts, the nickname "Spark Plug Lights" became popular. Orient Point Lighthouse in Long Island Sound has always worn the appropriate soubriquet of "CoffeePot."

caisson was then filled with compressed air, and on July 23rd had penetrated to a depth of 13 feet. On August 28 the required depth of 23 feet below the surface of the shoal was reached, and by the middle of September the contractors had finished the work of setting up the plates and filling into the cylinder 2,000 cubic yards of concrete.

Malley also explained that sinking the caisson into the bay floor required that two dozen men descend into the airlocked cylinder and dig the foundation. Sand was pumped out via a pipe. The men worked in the cylinder in eight-hour shifts and were paid two dollars a day, a princely sum at the time. The caisson settled to a depth of thirty-three feet and was further stabilized by riprap around its base. A temporary enclosure with a beacon was built atop the caisson in the autumn of 1885 to serve until the cast-iron house and lantern was completed in the spring of 1887. America had its first caisson lighthouses, and within a few years the style became commonplace.

As the nineteenth century wore on, the task of building lighthouses grew more technical, as did their maintenance. Simple lamps and fogbells had given way to labor-intensive machinery that required specialized training and more than a modicum of mechanical ability on the part of keepers. The flashing Fresnel lenses revolved using a clockworks system that had to be wound and maintained. Bell strikers powered by clockworks were introduced after the Civil War, followed by steam-powered horns in 1870. The light station foghouse was enlarged to accommodate coal-fired boilers to furnish steam and bellows to produce the ubiquitous honks. Sirens and whistles followed as the government sought the best sounds to penetrate the murk.

An equally important development was the debut of wireless communication. In September 1899, the revolutionary radio was demonstrated on the East Coast when a transmitter on a ship sent a 2,500-word message about the status of the America's Cup Race to a receiver at Navesink Twin Lights. Congress was so impressed with the invisible miracle, it appropriated twenty-five thousand dollars to install radios on all U.S. lighthouses and lightships, beginning with the most isolated. For families on isolated lighthouses and crews on lonely lightships, radios were lifelines. Lightkeepers could send and receive weather reports, easily monitor shipping, file status reports, and perhaps most importantly, connect with the shore in the event of an emergency.

The age of mechanized lightkeeping began with clockworks. These intricate systems automatically turned lenses and struck fogbells, freeing personnel for other duties. Gears had to be kept oiled, however, and winding up the weights suspended below the clockworks punctuated the lightkeeper's day. Most bells and striking mechanisms at mid-Atlantic lighthouses are quiet these days.

Administrative Changes

Much had been accomplished in a little over a century. By some estimates, as many as 1,400 lighthouses stood watch in the United States in 1900, their beams sweeping waters as far away as the territories of Alaska and Hawaii.

In 1896, President Grover Cleveland placed lighthouse employees under the Civil Service Act. No longer did politics determine who would keep a light. Written and oral exams were now required to get a job, a merit system was instituted for promotions, and rotation of duty within districts revitalized the system, allowing veteran keepers to train novices and lightkeepers to move through

Keepers of the Keepers

Far in the bosom of the deep
O'er these wild shelves my watch I keep;
A ruddy gleam of changeful light,
Bound on the brow of dusky night.
Sir Walter Scott, "Pharos Loquitur," 1814

Maintaining a few dozen lighthouses, fogbells, and buoys was an easy task for the early lighthouse service, but as the number of navigational aids grew it became evident a corps of vessels was needed to mind the lights and keep the keepers. The first lighthouse tender, as the workships were called, was the *Rush*. Purchased from the Revenue Cutter Service in 1840, it was assigned to the waters of the Northeast. Its task was to build and maintain lighthouses and lightships, provide logistical support, and provision lightkeepers from Maine to the Chesapeake Bay. In addition, *Rush* transported visitors, doctors, and teachers to lighthouses, delivered mail, and moved the keepers and their families from station to station.

By 1860, a number of lighthouse tenders were in service around the nation. About this time a curious tradition began that continued until the 1980s. Several vessels were purchased from the U.S. Navy's "flowerpot fleet," vessels with floral names in use during the Civil War. Among these were the *Iris*, *Geranium*, *Cactus*, and *Heliotrope*. The Lighthouse Board liked the cheerful names and began christening all its tenders for indigenous plants. Larger tenders were named for trees and shrubs and smaller vessels for flowers. A colorful fleet of sturdy tenders bloomed, homely in appearance, dirty in duty, but gently named. *Mistletoe* and *Tulip* worked the waters of Long Island Sound; *Dandelion*, *Sassafras*, and *Sunflower* served Philadelphia and the Delaware Bay and River. *Gardenia* was assigned to New York and Long Island, and *Holly*, *Thistle*, *Juniper*, *Bramble*, and *Woodbine* to the Chesapeake region. *Linden*, the first tender to have diesel electric engines, worked in the Norfolk area in the 1930s.

U.S. Lighthouse Tender (USLHT) *Maple* was typi-

The sidewheel lighthouse tender Holly *delivers supplies to lonely Point No Point Lighthouse in the Chesapeake Bay about 1900. Her lighthouse service ensign flies from the foremast and a visitor launch docks alongside. Delicate floral names notwithstanding, tenders like this one were the workhorses of the lighthouse service—building, repairing, and provisioning lighthouses, and caring for fog signals, buoys, and channel markers. (Photograph courtesy of the United States Coast Guard)*

cal. Built in 1892 at a cost of $93,888 by Samuel Moore & Sons at Elizabethport, New Jersey, she served the waters of the Chesapeake Bay from 1893 to 1933. The 164-foot long, black-hulled steam tender carried a crew of five to seven officers and twenty to twenty-five men. On her stern, in brass, were her name and a handsome lighthouse, emblem of the U.S. Lighthouse Board. She flew the triangular service flag from her foremast as well. Her primary duties included the support of lighthouses and lightships, fog signals, and buoys, but she also served as an inspection tender, transporting the district officer to conduct regular lighthouse inspections. At times, she performed beyond the call of duty. On January 15, 1914, under the command of Thomas J. Miles, *Maple* went to the aid of a powerless lumber schooner drifting dangerously off Cedar Point, Maryland. Lines were made fast, and the schooner was towed to safety.

Though the names of the tenders were delicate, their crews were not. These men of mettle—"tender boys"—were tough jacks-of-all-trades, as well as able-bodied seamen. Work was arduous and dangerous, often with the vessel pitching in the waves or precariously docked at a remote site. At a typical station, the men hauled sacks of coal from the tender to the lighthouse; filled the cistern with water; and carried tools, parts for the lantern and fog signal, containers of oil, and crates of food. They positioned buoys and channel markers and towed lightships on and off station. They hauled construction materials for new lighthouses and tore down or relocated others. It was rough work, but just as easily these strongmen could install a delicate lens or lift a mother and child in a breeches buoy and set them safely ashore.

After the Coast Guard absorbed the Lighthouse Service in 1939, buoy tenders gradually assumed the work of the old lighthouse tenders, keeping the tradition of botanical names. In the 1990s, the Coast Guard christened a new 175-foot "Keeper Class" of tenders that honor famous lightkeepers. Katie Walker, keeper of Robbins Reef Lighthouse from 1894 to 1919, is among fourteen heroes who lend their names to the new tenders. The *Katherine Walker* (WLM-552) was delivered to the Coast Guard on June 27, 1997, with great fanfare and is homeported in Bayonne, New Jersey—not far from where its diminutive namesake kept a light for ships headed into busy New York Harbor.

the ranks more easily. The lifestyle changed as well, to reflect the government's interest in keeping its civil servants happy. Tenders moved families and their possessions from light to light. Arrangements were made for the schooling of children at remote sites. Doctors and clergy regularly visited lighthouses. Portable libraries were circulated among the lighthouses and lightships to encourage education.

Attempts had been made throughout the second half of the nineteenth century to reorganize the system under the Navy Department or absorb it into other government agencies, but these had been parried with the simple justification that nothing ailed the Lighthouse Board. It had overhauled and modernized the service and elevated U.S. navigational aids to a level on par with the best in the world. What had operated almost as a cottage industry in the earliest years was now organized into a large government agency employing thousands and burdened with a massive budget.

Even so, some in Washington felt a change was due. The Lighthouse Board was too militaristic in its operations, and lighthouses by nature were structures of trade, not national defense. In 1903, the service again moved out of the Treasury Department and joined its compatriots—the U.S. Lifesaving Service and the U.S. Revenue Cutter Service—under the Department of Commerce and Labor. Within a decade, the Lighthouse Board was dissolved by the Organic Act of 1910, and management was again placed in civilian hands. Congress reasoned that the transience of military officers in charge of the various districts and on the Board itself failed to provide consistency and continuity.

A civilian chief heading a corps of permanent staff would rectify this problem, and the U.S. Bureau of Lighthouses was created in 1910. Its superintendent was George R. Putnam, a hard worker with a distinguished career with the U.S. Coast & Geodetic Survey. Over the next twenty-five years, he would gingerly move the service into the modern era. The Lighthouse Board had increased the number of lights from about 335 to nearly 4,000, fog signals from 50 to 450, and buoys from 1,000 to 5,300. Putnam would double those numbers while reducing personnel. The service was again on the verge of enormous change.

CHAPTER 4

The Modern Era

Left: *Evening sunlight burnishes the Hudson River around Hudson-Athens Lighthouse, the first beacon ships encounter on the route south from Albany. Built in 1874 to mark Middle Ground Flats, the elegant Second Empire tower was slow to be modernized, due to its insular location on a stone pier a quarter mile out in the river. Indoor plumbing came in 1938 and electricity in the 1940s. When modernization came in 1954, the lighthouse was automated and closed up.*

Above: *Roundout Lighthouse was automated in 1954, but a plastic optic installed in the 1980s made the station more self-sufficient, as did a solar panel. Coast Guard maintenance crews visit periodically to check the beacon and spruce up, but lack of fastidiousness is evidenced by paint spatters on the lens.*

The light I've tended for 40 years is now to be run
by a set of gears, the Keeper said.
And it isn't nice to be put ashore by a mere device.
Edgar Guest (1881–1959),
"The Lighthouse Keeper Wonders"

The lighthouse service moved into the twentieth century with considerably more confidence than it moved into the nineteenth. Backed by a well-trained and dedicated staff, it oversaw the world's best and most up-to-date system of navigational aids. There were nineteen districts stretching from Maine to Hawaii with the Mid-Atlantic itself encompassing three districts. In 1910, when the Bureau of Lighthouses was created to return the organization to civilian control, 1,462 lighthouses and 51 lightships were on duty, along with hundreds more minor beacons.

George R. Putnam, the first superintendent of the U.S. Bureau of Lighthouses, was in many ways as penny pinching as Stephen Pleasanton had been a century before, but he was also a man with a strong sense of fairness and a great affection for those in his service. Putnam carefully maintained public approval while keeping Washington bureaucrats satisfied. He managed to earn the respect and confidence of thousands of employees while cheerfully instilling a dedicated work ethic. Lightkeepers were encouraged to be patriotic and devoted to duty, with a philosophy of use it up, wear it out, and make it do. Paintbrushes were worn down to stubble, and pencils were ground until too small to grip. Lens cloths polished prisms and brass until tattered, then went into the keeper's wife's sewing basket for mending. Waste and indolence were abhorred, and frugality, initiative, and self-sacrifice were applauded.

Lightkeepers in the News

The U.S. *Lighthouse Service Bulletin*, a monthly in-house newsletter launched in 1912, became the venue for maintaining morale among lightkeepers, providing important information and news, as well as reporting instances of the aforementioned ideals. Putnam knew the value of both adulation and contrition. He noted examples of valor and honor in every issue.

1912: Frederick Lawson rescued a boy from drowning at Sunken Rock Light, New York. . . .
1913: William Davis of Lazaretto Light saved the Baltimore depot from catching fire when the lighthouse went up in flames. . . .

1930: Linwood Spicer retired after 35 years of devoted service as keeper of several Delaware lighthouses.

Keepers who earned the coveted annual Efficiency Pennant for their district were listed, including Ernest Bloom in 1912 for his work at Stepping Stones Light, E. H. Riggs at Cape Henry Light in 1913, John Berensten at Baltimore Light in 1914, and William Johnson at Bellevue Range Lights in 1931.

Disciplinary actions were reported equally. The March 1912 issue noted: "A lighthouse keeper has been reprimanded for misstatement of facts in conjunction with charges and for nagging of assistants." Reductions in rank and pay were noted, along with dismissals.

Accidents brought gentle admonitions. "The recent death of a keeper from asphyxiation emphasizes the importance of proper ventilation and proper care and attention to smoke pipes and flues," concluded a May 1934 entry. Putnam wasn't above proselytizing and often reminded employees of their duties as government servants and American citizens. Topics such as patriotism, punctuality, cleanliness, and carefulness were common.

Ingenuity was prized in Putnam's administration and shared with the entire service via the bulletin. Experiments in 1912 at the Portsmouth depot resulted in "devices designed to awaken lightkeepers when the light is burning too low." In 1934, the success of synchronized flashers tested at Christiana Range Lights outside Wilmington boasted that "all uncertainty on the part of the mariner as regards location and identity" was removed. Occasionally, the newsletter published a recipe or shared gardening tips. Astronomical events, such as eclipses, and unusual sea and weather phenomena of interest sprinkled the issues. The December 1934 bulletin carried an uplifting poem by Douglas Malloch, the last verse noting:

The lighthouse has no special friends,
No special foes, when night descends.
In all the earth the only place,
Though statesmen talk and kings embrace,
Where man becomes one common race.

The result of Putnam's efforts was a more unified and efficient service. Over the twenty-seven years the U.S. *Lighthouse Service Bulletin* was published, resignations and disciplinary actions declined and morale soared. The number of navigational aids doubled, and the service moved into an age of tightly organized man-

Lamps and tools in a lighthouse workroom just below the lantern recall a bygone era when human hands tended old oil lamps and keepers were lauded for their beneficent work. A variety of tools were specially made for the job, and their use was detailed in Instructions to Lightkeepers, *a service manual first published by the U.S. Lighthouse Board in the 1850s.*

agement, automation, and modernization. Without realizing, Putnam, whose mission was to civilianize the lighthouse service, prepared it for a return to military leadership under the U.S. Coast Guard in 1939.

An Era of Growth and Improvements

Putnam's penchant for good publicity brought the benevolent work of the Lighthouse Service into public view in his many radio interviews, speeches, and writings. A 1913 issue of *National Geographic* included an extensive article by Putnam edifying and demystifying the work of the Bureau of Lighthouses. It assured everyone that, though he was a civilian with no experience in navigation, he had done his homework. At this time, 1,733 lightkeepers were on duty around the nation, about 350 of them along the mid-Atlantic shores. Of their dedication Putnam affectionately penned: "Although the pay is small and the life often lonely, the work attracts as a rule an excellent class of faithful men, willing to take large risks in doing their duty and also in helping those in distress." He cited the keeper of Van Weis Point Light in New York who had recently died "at the age of 93 years, having tended this light for 52 years." The article was lavishly illustrated. Among the images were a diagram of the pneumatic process used to build Fourteen Foot Bank Lighthouse, a photo of the fog signal house at Cape Henry Light with its trumpet-shaped sirens spouting steam, and a panoramic view of the large depot at Staten Island.

Leading Putnam's early agenda

was the rebuilding of many screwpile lighthouses. The old iron tower at Brandywine Shoal was showing its age and expensive to maintain. In 1911, Congress appropriated $75,000 for a new design better suited to the exposed waters of the Delaware Bay. Reinforced concrete, the popular material of the day, served well, though some aesthetics found it less than pleasing to the eye. A concrete tower also replaced the screwpile lighthouse at Thimble Shoal, which had burned in 1909. In 1912, Lloyd Harbor Lighthouse on Long Island Sound became the first land light on the East Coast built of reinforced concrete.

Keeping a large station like Cape Henry shipshape was not easy, particularly before the advent of electricity. Lightkeeper E. H. Riggs, who earned a coveted Efficiency Pennant in 1913, would have spent much of his day cleaning the tower's huge first-order lens and carrying fuel up to the lantern.

World War I saw the Bureau of Lighthouses transfer to the U.S. War Department and the lighthouse keepers and lightship crews placed on alert. Lightships maintained special watches, and tenders moved up and down the coast with care. The creation of the U.S. Coast Guard in 1915 increased coastal defense with more beach patrols and policing of waters, and lighthouse keepers often found themselves among the fraternity of lookouts and beachpounders of nearby lifesaving stations.

In October 1918, an accident at a munitions plant at Morgan, New Jersey, shook the ground and sent shrapnel screaming over three lighthouses. Old Orchard Light and Princes Bay Light reported minor damage, but at Great Beds Lighthouse the keeper feared for his life and sent his family to shore on Staten Island. Earth-shaking explosions caused the iron tower to shudder, breaking glass in the lantern and putting out the light. Red-hot cinders whistled through the air, threatening the kerosene tanks. Fortunately, the lighthouse escaped conflagration.

A high point came late in the war when Putnam secured a long-awaited benefit for his employees. In 1916, he had noted with concern that ninety-two keepers employed by the bureau were over the age of seventy. The reason for the longevity was that no pension plan existed. By 1918, the situation had changed. Employees with thirty years of service could retire with a full pension at age sixty-five, and mandatory retirement came at age seventy. Hundreds of keepers gratefully sent in resignations. President Woodrow Wilson commented to Putnam after passage of the bill, "I know how important their work is and feel that nothing but justice has been done them." Such accolades for the keepers were important at a time when many felt the government's rush to modernize the service might supercede the need for them.

Invisible Signals and Flickers of Automation

Toward the end of World War I, Putnam moved the lighthouse service to the forefront of research in new signaling techniques and direction finding. In 1917, the light-

George Putnam, Superintendent of the U.S. Bureau of Lighthouses from 1910 to 1935, moved lighthouse technology into the modern era with projects such as Long Island Sound's Lloyd Harbor Lighthouse, the first land light on the East Coast constructed of reinforced concrete. Critics dubbed it unsightly and an insult to traditional lighthouse architecture, but Putnam called it practical, since it was easier to build and maintain than a masonry tower. Its success in 1912 made concrete a staple of lighthouse construction in the twentieth century.

house tender *Tulip* tried out an experimental radio compass to locate a radio fog signal transmitter at Navesink Twin Lights. The successful experiment resulted in the installation of radio transmitters at three Chesapeake Bay lights in 1919, plus the gift of a radio compass for the tender *Arbutus*. The first radiobeacon antennas were placed at the Sea Girt and Fire Island lighthouses and on Ambrose Lightship to provide a triangulation grid in which ships could fix position. By 1940, such forms of silent signaling were commonplace, with some 150 stations equipped with radiobeacons.

In the 1920s, aviators joined mariners in using the lighthouses as navigational aids. The Lighthouse Service established its Airways Division in 1926 to share the guiding lights of the coasts with pilots, thus helping move mail, passengers, and cargo more effectively. Skeleton towers mounted with powerful searchlights were built in more than 1,500 locations. Lighthouses were painted with numbers and letters to help air traffic move

Overleaf: With the addition of the Airways Division in 1926, the role of the lighthouse service expanded greatly. Aviators had been using lighthouses as guideposts for years, but the addition of searchlights and a numbering system for daytime identification were a boon. Cape May Lighthouse on the New Jersey side of the ingress of the Delaware Bay was an important aid for aircraft headed to Philadelphia. Fliers picked up its beacon at sea, then ran the bay's north shore following the string of lights at Brandywine Shoal, Miah Maull, Elbow of Cross Ledge, and Ship John Shoal.

up and down the coast in the daytime. Landfall beacons at sites such as Montauk Point, Navesink, Cape May, Cape Charles, and Assateague proved invaluable guides in rapidly crowding skies. By 1934, the task of maintaining so many airway beacons had grown too large for the Lighthouse Service and was transferred to the Federal Aviation Administration.

Meanwhile, better methods of illumination continued to be developed. Electricity was a cleaner and quicker source of light, but it also brought a plethora of contraptions—power lines, power plants, fuses, switches, bulbs, wires—all wanting attention. It also brought the all-too-frequent nuisance of outages. Oil lamps were kept as backup, and keepers remained familiar with both systems.

Electricity was slow to arrive at many remote and offshore stations, and often it was only the beacon that was electrified, while keepers and their families continued to light their homes with oil lamps. Navesink Twin Lights had its own electric power plant in 1898, yet the keeper's quarters remained unwired until the 1930s. Underwater cables had to be laid to screwpile and caisson lighthouses and those on islands. Lights of lesser importance were far down the list. Turkey Point Lighthouse in the Chesapeake Bay was not electrified until 1944, probably because its keeper was content to tend the old oil lamps.

Electric generators were common. The conversion at Assateague Lighthouse in 1933, its hundredth anniversary, reflected the expansive modernization campaign. Its 1866 first-order Fresnel lens, burning kerosene, gave way to an electric beacon. The new generators powered three 1,000-watt bulbs controlled by a timer that turned them on and off at appropriate times. The system doubled the candlepower of the lighthouse. Despite the laborsaving updates, Assateague Lighthouse remained manned until 1965, owing to its importance as a landfall beacon and community concern about a human presence on the lonely station.

Putnam saw a great future in a robotic, self-sufficient corps of navigational aids, but he moved cautiously on the issue, knowing the public felt otherwise, as did many mariners. Among the first stations to be unmanned was East Point Light guarding the Maurice River. Its successful 1911 conversion led to others: Pooles Island Light went automatic in 1917, Jones Point Light in 1919, Concord Point Light in 1920.

The U.S. Lighthouse Service Bulletin for September 1925 proudly reported the benefits of these changes: "During the year ended June 30, 1925, lights were changed to automatic at 74 stations at a total cost of $50,748, and this resulted in the reduction of annual operating cost of $17,785." The report went on to say that "the reduction of keepers was made without serious hardship . . . by filling vacancies at other stations by transfer." Few realized that a multitude of employees in the service might shrink dramatically over the coming decades before disappearing entirely, or that modernization would permanently destroy or alter many historic buildings. The nation, infatuated with its own sense of technological superiority, embraced Putnam's vision of an automated service.

The drawbacks soon became clear as the grandeur of many old lighthouses was displaced by pile towers and stark steel skeletons. In 1928, Block Island, south of the entrance to Philadelphia's Schuykill River, was christened with a thirty-foot steel tower, and two years later another one was built at the river entrance. Where quaint old Ludlam Beach Lighthouse once stood in New Jersey was now a graceless steel structure. Such lights were found on remote sites and in the far-flung islands of Alaska and Hawaii, but in the heart of America, where rugged colonial light towers still majestically kept watch, no framework of metal and wires could be called a "lighthouse." The public recoiled and called them monstrous "Erector Sets." Beacons themselves also changed as industrial lights began to engulf the shoreline. The warm golden rays of coastal sentinels began to give way to blue-white beams and rapid flashes.

About this same time, whispers of preservation began to be heard. Putnam posted metal signs at unattended and abandoned lighthouses warning vandals of the consequences of damage to lighthouse property. Despite the advantages of his automation agenda, he

Turkey Point Lighthouse on Elk Neck in the Chesapeake Bay was one of the last in the nation to be electrified. Its aging last keeper, Fanny Salter, lit both the lantern and her house with oil lamps from 1924 to 1944 while many of her compatriots enjoyed modern conveniences. The station's isolation and Salter's reclusive nature probably contributed to the slow updating of equipment. Salter enjoyed the carefree benefits of electricity only three years before retiring in 1947.

Roundout Lighthouse at Kingston, New York, seems to float on the Hudson River on a pleasant autumn day. Offshore lights like this one were among the earliest to be automated, owing to the difficulties of keeping their resident crews provisioned and content.

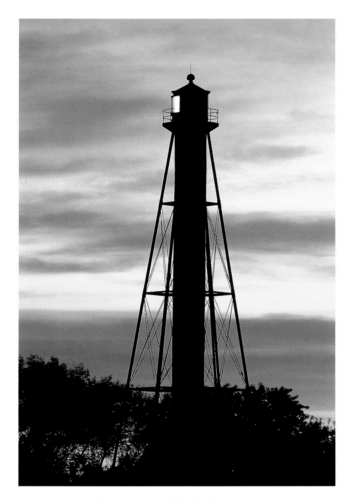

Facing page: The cottage-style lighthouse at East Point, New Jersey, was the first in the Mid-Atlantic to be automated. Though not the most remote lighthouse in the region, its distance from town was a hardship for its keepers. Removal of resident personnel was cost effective and sensible at such sites, but vandalism and deterioration were drawbacks. Abandoned entirely in 1941, the lighthouse deteriorated miserably before the Maurice River Historical Society assumed care of it in the 1980s.

Above: *The definition of "lighthouse" is hotly debated. Any structure surmounted by a navigational light and large enough to be occupied by a resident keeper might be called a lighthouse, but critics pan the stark metallic visage of pile and skeleton towers. Liston Rear Range Light at Port Penn, Delaware, is often mistaken for a water tower, but its mission is decidedly navigational. It is one of a pair of beacons that act as a range for ships inside the Delaware River channel.*

was distressed at the loss of the historic buildings and looked to private groups as a means of relieving the bureau "of the embarrassing situation of being called upon to use its funds for a purpose for which they were not appropriated—the preservation of an historical monument."

During the Depression-era economy, there was little interest in stewardship of orphaned lighthouses, but a few found homes. The old Cape Henry Lighthouse, long obsolete and needing care, was among the first. Transferred to the Association for the Preservation of Virginia Antiquities in 1930, its door was left unlocked to allow visitor access. Naturally, the elements and vandalism began to take a toll. The City of Virginia Beach, which had adopted the lighthouse for its seal, formed a partnership with the association by taking over maintenance of the historic tower. A lock went on the door when tours were not in progress.

At George Putnam's retirement in 1935, he was lauded for accomplishments above and beyond what could be expected during World War I and the Great Depression. Harold King, who had served under him as a district manager and deputy commissioner, became the new Commissioner of Lighthouses. King had hardly begun his own program of updating and streamlining the service when, in July 1939, President Franklin D. Roosevelt implemented a government Reorganization Plan II, which transferred the Bureau of Lighthouses to the U.S. Coast Guard. The Navy Department was displeased. Its strong ties to lighthouses dated back to the formation of the Lighthouse Board in 1852. That a service so old should fall under the aegis of the Coast Guard, an organization that had been in existence only twenty-four years, seemed incongruous. Congress was adamant, however, that lighthouses belonged with other commerce and trade agencies, not those of national defense. The merger increased Coast Guard personnel from 10,000 to 17,000 and absorbed some 29,000 aids to navigation.

The transfer took place only a few weeks before a planned grand celebration of the 150th anniversary of the lighthouse service on August 7, 1939. To palliate disappointment, President Roosevelt declared the first week of August as "Lighthouse Week" in honor of the consolidation of the two essential maritime agencies. Lightkeepers were given the choice of continuing in civil service or transferring to Coast Guard ranks, usually as chiefs or first-class petty officers. By 1940, a 10 percent savings of the lighthouse service's annual budget had

Many lighthouses were dimmed or extinguished during World War II to prevent them from silhouetting ships at sea and making them easy targets for U-boats. Barnegat Inlet Lighthouse appears serene on a sunny summer day, but on a similar day in 1944 keepers watched fearfully as a tanker exploded after being torpedoed by a German submarine and fire raged over the sea.

been realized, but not everyone was pleased. Light-keepers, many of whom were approaching retirement, had difficulty serving with youthful comrades and answering to superiors half their age. As expected, there was dissension over styles of work and, too often, resentment that a military organization had replaced a civilian one.

Lighthouses in World War II

Before arguments could heat up, the nation was thrust into war again, uniting active duty and civilian duties under one cause. The Coast Guard became a wartime agency operating under the Navy Department. As a matter of national security, major seacoast lights were extinguished or switched to low power so their beams did not silhouette ships and make them easy targets for U-boats. A system of radio communications called ANRAC advised keepers when lights needed to be turned on, and they, in turn, maintained regular contact with district headquarters to report sightings of enemy vessels or other problems. Those in more vulnerable areas were given rifles and marksmanship training. Unattended lighthouses were operated by radio signals from remote control stations. Coast Guard patrols and lookouts began at or near more than fifty lighthouses between Long Island and the Outer Banks.

A local resident near Sea Girt Lighthouse described the wartime atmosphere: "The beaches were patrolled by men on foot and sometimes with dogs. A constant radio watch was kept and sailors with binoculars always manned the tower. They would see the flash of light, hear the terrible roar of a tanker being blown up by torpedo attack and all they could do was report and watch. The beach was littered with ship's wreckage, rafts and fuel oil."

Not far from Montauk Point Light, beach patrols at Amagansett captured four Nazi saboteurs. The lightkeepers later saw an American pilot ditch his disabled plane in the sea off the point and called for help. At Coney Island Light the crew found mines washed ashore near a populated area and stood guard over them until a special ordnance team removed the danger. Swimming areas were closed as patrols and lookouts increased. Those that remained open were heavily guarded. The keeper at Assateague Lighthouse heard the explosion of a freighter being sunk offshore by an enemy submarine and assisted the Coast Guard with rescue efforts.

Ugly Duckling Lighthouses

*T*inicum Rear Range Light isn't beautiful, at least not by lighthouse standards. It looks like a giant coffee can held aloft by black steel legs wearing concrete shoes. No fabulous ocean vistas are seen from its lantern, no sandy beaches at its feet. The view from here is decidedly industrial. Even the Delaware River channel seems remote, glimpsed beyond trees, houses, a Little League ball field, and an oil refinery. For years, the people of Paulsboro, New Jersey, saw nothing remarkable about their lighthouse. Many thought it was a water tower.

All that changed when Myles and Alice Hillary decided the 1880 Tinicum Rear Range Light was worth saving. Lighthouses hold special significance for them. They were married at Maine's Portland Head Lighthouse and volunteer as tour guides at Sandy Hook Lighthouse. When they saw Tinicum Light for the first time, they knew it had a story to tell. Alice Hillary explains: "There was a man hitting golf balls at it, using it for a target. We realized people didn't know this is a lighthouse, a piece of living history."

Tinicum is a special kind of lighthouse called a "range." It belongs to a class of navigational aids that form the backbone of channel navigation. A range consists of a pair of lights called "upper" and "lower," or "rear" and "front." The lower, or front, beacon sits at a lower elevation than the upper, or rear, beacon. A ship steers so that the pair of range lights appear piggyback and thus keeps a safe course in the channel. Once called "leading lights," ranges were introduced in America at Savannah, Georgia, in 1820 and were a regular feature on inland waterways by 1850.

Tinicum Light is among several sets of ranges that bring ships in and out of Philadelphia. Though only the tower stands today, it was once a pastoral station with a house, small barn, fruit trees, and white picket fence. Families lived here. Curtains hung at the windows, the aromas of bread and roast beef wafted from the kitchen, wash flapped on the clothesline, and children played on the lawn. The lighthouse was not glamorous or majestically perched on a scenic headland, nor did its beacon shine any great distance. Duty at such a lighthouse may seem lackluster, but when added to the overall mission of waterway safety, the work was crucial. The Tinicum lightkeepers performed an important humanitarian service.

The Hillarys convinced Coast Guard officials in Philadelphia to open Tinicum Light to the public on Paulsboro Day, 1997.

"They were skeptical about there being any interest, but they came out and did a professional job," said Alice Hillary. "I think they were very surprised at the turnout."

More than 1,200 people climbed the tower that day and heard its history. Dave Birch, a grandson of the last lightkeeper, chatted with visitors and shared family pictures. Paulsboro's retired police chief, Ray Miller, set up an easel and painted the lighthouse as it might have looked in its attended years. A donation box quickly filled with dollars. The Tinicum Rear Range Light Society was incorporated that same year, the first group in the Mid-Atlantic devoted to saving a range light.

Most of today's range lights are modern steel towers with little aesthetic appeal, but a few older examples still stand. In New York, Sandy Hook Bay's Chapel Hill Rear Range Light, decommissioned in 1940, and the New Dorp Range Light that marked the Swash Channel approach to New York Harbor until 1964, are old-style wooden beacons now privately owned. Still active is the Ambrose Channel range formed by the comely brick Staten Island Light and the cast-iron West Bank Light.

Among New Jersey's older range lights is Finns Point Rear Range Light at Penns Neck, established in 1877. The dangers at this point in the river are underscored by the fact that 147 vessels of all sizes wrecked here between 1926 and 1934, and keeper F. C. Hill received sixteen lifesaving commendations. Finns Point Rear Range Light served until 1950 when widening of the channel necessitated a new alignment, and the Reedy Island Range Lights on the Delaware side of the channel took over the job. Delaware is also home to the Liston Rear Range Light, built in 1878 at Port Penn and moved to the entrance of the Chesapeake and Delaware Canal in 1904. The 1909 Bellevue Rear Range Light at the entrance to the Christiana River gave up its job to a steel skeleton tower in 2001 after a nearby landfill had grown so tall the light became obscured.

The Chesapeake Bay's best-known range lights are those of Baltimore's Craighill Channel. Named for William Price Craighill, a longtime servant of the Lighthouse Board, this intricate waterway is a shortcut that leads from the Chesapeake Bay into the Patapsco River by way of the Brewerton Channel. Two sets of ranges—four lights in all—were established here, the first in 1873 in the lower portion of the channel, then a second set in 1886 in its upper reaches. The lights have operated automatically since 1964.

Thousands of range lights safeguard the waterways of the nation, doing the most critical work of all navigational aids. Yet they are the unsung beacons of lighthouse history, forgotten largely because of their humble appearance.

"We don't pretend our lighthouse is beautiful," says Alice Hillary of Tinicum Rear Range Light Society. "We love it for other reasons. I guess you could call it an ugly duckling lighthouse."

Affection for old abandoned lighthouses runs high these days, even for a homely metal hulk like Tinicum Rear Range Light. The citizens of Paulsboro, New Jersey, love their 1880 lighthouse and have made it the focus of a town festival that draws thousands of visitors. Anyone energetic enough to climb up the 112 steps to the top of the eighty-five-foot wrought-iron tower is rewarded with a panoramic view of the Delaware River.

Chesapeake Lightship, normally anchored fourteen miles off Virginia Beach, was fitted with 20mm guns and enlisted in the Navy as a patrol boat, keeping watch on U-boat activity along the mid-Atlantic coast. The lighthouse keepers at Cape Charles and Smith Island shared watches with Coast Guard patrols and their well-trained dogs; these pristine islands of the Eastern Shore seemed likely spots for subversive enemy activities. German submarine "wolf packs" torpedoed numerous tankers within sight and sound of the lightkeepers of the Virginia capes in 1942. The *Rochester* sank off Cape Henry in January, followed by the *E. H. Blum* in February, the *Oakmar* in March, and the freighters *Robin Hood* and *Alcoa Skipper* in April. Lighthouse and lightship personnel radioed for help with each sinking and assisted with rescues.

New Age Navigation

After the war, the Coast Guard returned to the Department of Commerce and resumed modernization of its navigational aids. A problem of growing concern was the tableau of city lights that surrounded many lighthouses, making identification difficult. Old Point Comfort Light was among the first to be floodlighted in 1956; the floodlighting cost $350 and helped the lighthouse show up against the skyline of Newport News, Virginia. The effect was also aesthetically charming, placing the lighthouse in the spotlight each evening and luring hordes of photographers eager for a shot of its nocturnal beauty.

The use of exterior lighting was on the rise, but the beacons were also undergoing more significant internal change. Smaller, more durable lighting mechanisms were developed, lights that employed the same catadioptric principles as the old classical lenses but with a new miracle material. Plastic was cheap to manufacture, required little maintenance, and held up well in the exposed conditions at lighthouses. Plastic lenses began to supersede Fresnel lenses. Compact and durable, they could easily run on their own for months at a time. Lightkeepers had evolved from wickies tending oil lamps to switchies daily turning on and off beacons and horns with a single stroke of the finger. Now they could leave the work to robot keepers.

By 1940, nearly thirty mid-Atlantic lighthouses had gone automatic, all successful experiments in self-sufficient operation. Putnam's early twentieth-century vision now proceeded in earnest. Offshore lights, where housing personnel was expensive or immediate upgrades were needed, were among the first to be converted. The lighthouses at Hudson-Athens and Huntington Harbor, New York, were automated in 1949 and Orient Point and Roundout in 1954. Thimble Shoal and Newport News Middle Ground in Hampton Roads also were unmanned in 1954, and Old Orchard the next year. Keepers departed Bloody Point Bar, Drum Point, and Solomons Lump in the Chesapeake in 1960.

The effort stepped up in the mid 1960s with the Coast Guard's Lighthouse Automation and Modernization Program (LAMP). Reliable timers and sensors developed to deal with varying light and fog levels quickly became the backbone of automation. An array of high-tech gadgets automatically ran lights and fog signals, rotated new bulbs into position when old ones burned out, and activated backup systems if the lights and horns failed. Solar batteries powered many of the remote stations, while computerized monitoring systems within each district alerted the Coast Guard if a problem arose. Even an "Atomic Lighthouse," with a sixty-watt isotopic generator cell supplying electricity, was tested in 1964 at Baltimore Light; the concept worked but was abandoned due to cost and environmental concerns.

The occupation of lighthouse keeper was fast becoming obsolete. Critics bemoaned the removal of a human presence, saying an automatic lighthouse could not answer a ship in distress or rescue someone drowning. Who would wash the lantern windows and groom the grounds? Who would greet visitors and give tours? Without keepers on site, lighthouse efficiency dropped to 95 percent. Yet because the cost of automation paid for itself at each lighthouse within four years and freed up Coast Guard personnel to work at other more critical jobs, a loss of 5 percent efficiency seemed a small compromise.

By 1995, all but one U.S. lighthouse had been automated. Boston Light—the nation's first official beacon—remained attended for nostalgia's sake. Even there, automatic devices ran the station and required no assistance from the figurehead crew.

Lighthouses had become their own keepers.

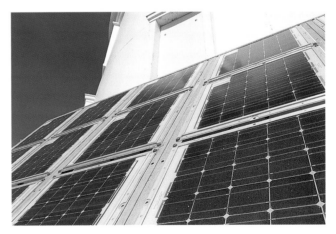

Twentieth-century technology at Brandywine Shoal Lighthouse in the Delaware Bay has made the station self-sufficient and rendered the job of lightkeeper obsolete in a sense, though Coast Guard Aids to Navigation Teams (ANT) still visit about twice a year and perform many housekeeping and mechanical tasks. The modern Vega VRB-25 optic (above, right) has its bugs and dirt cleaned away and electrical connections and bulbs checked. Windows are washed and any cracks where water and salt can intrude are caulked. An array of fifteen solar panels (right) powering the beacon and dual foghorns (above) are inspected, too. All this high-tech gadgetry adds a cluttered look to the lighthouse's weather deck and lantern, but it negates the need for resident keepers.

A *haunt for seabirds, the granite pier foundation of Cross Ledge Lighthouse (below) now serves only as a daymark and icebreaker in the Delaware Bay five miles off the town of Port Mahon, Delaware. The handsome 1877 wood frame house that once stood atop the pier was abandoned in 1910 after a long travail with storm and ice damage. It deteriorated slowly until World War II when the military acquired it for aircraft target practice. Bombers from Naval Air Station Wildwood, New Jersey, left the lighthouse in sad shape. Its remains were burned by the Coast Guard in 1962.*

Meanwhile, its successor at nearby Elbow of Cross Ledge had gone into service in 1910 staffed by the three keepers who had transferred from defunct Cross Ledge. Their littoral home at Elbow of Cross Ledge Lighthouse consisted of a triple-tier, octagonal, brick and iron house atop an iron caisson. A fourth-order Fresnel lens and 2,000-pound fogbell provided the signals for the station.

Elbow of Cross Ledge Lighthouse served an uneventful tenure until October 1953 when it was hit by a passing freighter during a morning fog. No one was injured, since the lighthouse had been automated and unmanned two years before, but the upper tiers of the tower were pushed overboard into the bay. The buoy tender Lilac promptly sank several buoys around the site until a new light could be completed. The remains of the ruined lighthouse were razed, and a steel skeleton tower was erected in its place. The tower remains on duty, showing a white beacon with a red sector to mark shoals on the east side of the channel. Its iron caisson shell (above) wears the station name to help ships identify it during the day.

THE TEXAS TOWERS

Over the centuries, lighthouses have evolved through many architectural forms, some more aesthetically pleasing than others. Rugged masonry towers are familiar favorites, but this design was not suitable for every site. In places where lighthouses stood in water, special structures were used, and the deeper the site, the more challenging the design.

This was surely the case at two waterbound stations off the Chesapeake Bay and New York Harbor. Here engineers in the 1960s constructed state-of-the-art sentinels based on offshore oilrig designs. Known as Texas towers, they are the Mid-Atlantic's newest lighthouses.

Chesapeake Offshore Light Structure, christened in 1965 to replace the old Chesapeake Lightship, was the first. Standing in forty-two feet of water some fourteen miles east of the bay, it was built by the same company that constructed the Chesapeake Bay Bridge and Tunnel. Its blue tubular legs and square white light tower soon became a familiar and welcome greeting to ships headed into the nation's biggest estuary. A rotating crew of six Coast Guard keepers watched over the dual-intensity, six-million-candlepower beacon until the station was automated in 1980.

A Texas tower–style lighthouse replaced collision-vulnerable Ambrose Lightship in August 1967, some seven miles off Sandy Hook, New Jersey. The $2.4 million struc-ture stood in seventy-five feet of water on four forty-two-inch-diameter legs driven 170-feet into the seafloor. The crew quarters were ninety feet above the waterline, with a forty-six-foot tall tower rising from the helicopter deck. Like its sister sentinel at Chesapeake, Ambrose Light had six keepers, with four always on duty. Michael St. John, who served at the light from 1983 to 1984, remembered how frightening the duty was on murky days: "During my stay at Ambrose I acquired a permanent dislike of fog at sea. Often, a ship would come by so close that we could hear its engines, smell the exhaust, and see the wake of its passing but never see the vessel itself."

Even in clear weather the tower was at risk of being hit. On October 5, 1996, the oil tanker *Aegeo* struck one of the legs after straying off course. Fortunately, the light had been automated and the keepers removed in 1988, so no one was on board to experience the terror of the collision. The crippled light station was left standing on three legs. Offshore Specialty Fabricators of Louisiana built a new Texas tower in 1998 and removed the damaged one. Four piles were driven deep into the seabed, then the superstructure was brought out by barge and lifted onto the legs. Similar to its predecessor, the new Ambrose Light Tower was painted bright red to make it easily visible to ships.

Historic Ambrose Lightship surrendered her position at Ambrose Station, located seven miles off New York Harbor, to the ultra-modern Texas tower–style lighthouse in 1967. The lightship was retired to the South Street Seaport Museum in New York City. The Texas tower was struck by a tanker in 1996 and had to be rebuilt. (Photograph courtesy of the United States Coast Guard)

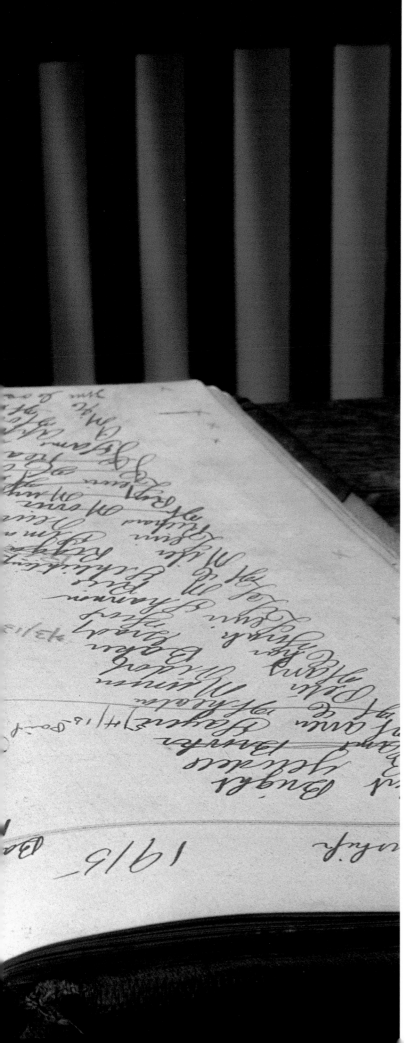

CHAPTER 5

The Old Keepers

Left: *The station logbook preserved a record of the daily activities at lighthouses. Keepers, for the most part, wrote terse and colorless entries about chores, weather, personnel changes, and visitors. Occasionally, a poet put his pen to work. Charles Sterling, keeper of Hog Island Lighthouse in Virginia colorfully described the local wildlife, noting, "Indeed nature has so bountifully endowed Hog Island that it discounts the fabled island of Calypso!"*

Above: *A rocking chair on the porch at Piney Point Lighthouse in Maryland suggests the lightkeeper had a leisure life. Spare time was at a premium at most mainland stations, however.*

*I notice how the monotony of a quiet life stimulates
the creative mind. Certain callings in our modern
organization entail such a life. I think of such
occupations as the service in the lighthouses.*
Albert Einstein, *Out of My Later Years*, 1950

Lighthouse keepers had been on government payrolls keeping the shores brightly lit for 279 years when the last personnel were relieved of duty. Like medieval knights and the cowboys of the Old West, they faded into history. It happened so gradually the nation hardly seemed to notice. Lighthouses still looked the same, standing cathedral-like over the shore, and most continued to beam each night. But something spiritual was missing.

Bob Garrett, the Coast Guard officer who oversaw the final lighthouse automations, sensed the public's feeling of loss at the close of the twentieth century: "It's all about the traditional definition of the word *lighthouse*. *House* suggests that someone ought to live there, and these structures certainly served as homes for many years. The lighthouse keeper people love—the one they see in old, yellowed photos—disappeared long ago, long before LAMP."

Exactly when lighthouse keepers disappeared is debatable. The official date is 1995, but obsolescence characterized them long before that. Perhaps when the nightly duties of lighting up the oil lamps went away so did the traditional role. And with it went the popular archetype—the wise and gentle soul, white-whiskered, leather-faced, hobbling about on retired sea legs with a cat for company, preferably one he'd rescued from a shipwreck. He trimmed the wicks, struck the match, and spent much of his time sitting by a window watching for ships in distress, reading into the deep hours of night, or making ships in bottles. Few keepers fit this quixotic ideal, but it is the one we cherish.

Old Salts on Watch

Early lightkeepers, almost without exception, were chosen from surrounding communities and often owned the land where a lighthouse stood. They tended the light as a sideline to farming, fishing, or other jobs.

Thomas Dickinson was typical. The government wanted to build range lights on his property at Finns Point on the Delaware River in the 1870s. Dickinson agreed to sell only if he got the job as keeper.

War heroes and crippled veterans also were considered good lightkeeping candidates. Noah Mason, a Revolutionary War hero and resident of Long Island, petitioned New York Senator Samuel Mitchell to have a lighthouse built on Sands Point. Apparently, his argument was tenable and he had the proper connections, for the tower was completed in 1809, and he was appointed the light's first keeper. Captain Charles Mulford lost a leg in the Civil War, then received an appointment to Cedar Island Light on Long Island as propitiation for his infirmity, patriotically incurred in support of the Union cause. Long after he departed, his wooden leg was found gathering dust in the lighthouse attic. Local war hero and favorite citizen John O'Neill was the first keeper of Concord Point Light. His appointment came, no doubt, as a result of his popularity in the community. He had thwarted a British attack on the town of Havre de Grace in 1813, been taken prisoner, and faced hanging until the charms of his daughter softened a British admiral's heart and got him released. Freeling Hewitt, the second keeper at New Jersey's Hereford Inlet Lighthouse, had fought in the Civil War, and lighthouse duty must have seemed a reward for the service. He stayed at his post for forty-five years.

Politics played an important role in who got the job. "Mr. Lawrence was a faithful, capable man," the Sandwich *Register* reported in 1854 after the dismissal of a lightkeeper. "His crime consisted in having been appointed by the Whigs." With the election of Abraham Lincoln in 1860, 70 percent of lightkeepers in the nation lost their jobs. A keeper's logbook grimly noted in October 1885: "Received my discharge as keeper of Cape Henry Lighthouse on account of being a Republican." Such favoritism didn't end until the 1890s.

There was no minimum or maximum age for lighthouse keepers in the early years, nor did they need special training. Until the U.S. Lighthouse Board assumed control in 1852, lightkeepers were not required to be literate, keep records of their work, be able to swim and

The word "lighthouse" suggests an occupant, and indeed, lighthouses were built with a dual purpose as navigational aids and as homes for the people who tended them. The keeper's house was sometimes within the tower itself, as was the case at most offshore assignments, but more often it was a structure separate from the tower. On mainland stations there was usually ample room for a large family. Horton Point Lighthouse was typical. Its spacious quarters are attached to the tower, making access easy for the keeper on a cold or stormy night. A large porch faces the lawn and Long Island Sound.

A nineteenth-century landmark struggles to shine in the modern world. Absecon Lighthouse and its steadfast keepers stood a lonely watch over the sands of southern New Jersey before Atlantic City sprang up. Today, the glare of casinos and hotels nearly washes out its ceremonial beacon.

handle a boat, or undergo inspections. Not until 1882 were uniforms prescribed to foster pride and esprit de corps.

With so much work to do and the loneliness that often came with the job, the service encouraged married men to apply. Rejected bachelors were sometimes advised to reapply when married, which sent more than one man in search of a sturdy bride. Lightkeeping was often a family affair handed down generation to generation. The Hoose family served a total of fifty years at Coxsackie Light on the Hudson River, and the Murdocks attended neighboring Roundout Lighthouse from 1855 to 1922. Jonathan Miller and his son served at Montauk Point Light for a total of sixty years. Wives sometimes took over after their husbands died. The lighthouse service felt widows and grown children were trained adequately and familiar with their stations, and it was cost effective to appoint them rather than transfer in another keeper.

A Diverse Duty

Time and place defined the lightkeepers' work. Assignments varied from pastoral land lights and island stations, where life was much like a small farm with the added duty of a beacon; to inland bay and river lights; to large, sea-swept landfall towers where families were surrounded by water as if on a ship eternally at anchor. Stations that were remote when first built sometimes ended up in the sprawl of urban streets. Fenwick Island's lightkeepers were virtually cut off from civilization for the first twenty years. To reach the closest town a wagon had to be pulled by scow across Fenwick Ditch. Turnover of personnel was high. Many keepers resigned, citing the station as too isolated. When a bridge linked the island with the mainland in 1880, Ocean City sprang up. By 1950, the lighthouse was lost in the glare of hotel, restaurant, and shop lights. Absecon Light, discontinued in 1933, experienced a similar adjustment when Atlantic City became a popular vacation destination.

On waterbound lighthouses, keepers experienced the pangs of separation from their families and mainland comforts. Katie Walker was determined to live with her husband in the 1880s on Robbins Reef Light in the middle of New York Harbor but grew heartsick at the "sight of water everywhere I look." She refused to unpack her suitcase for months. She grew to like the cloistered life, however; she raised two children on the lighthouse and succeeded her husband as keeper. By the time the Coast Guard took over lighthouses in 1939, wives weren't allowed to live on "stag stations," as offshore assignments were called. Keeper Bill Johnson's wife drove the family car to the shores of the Delaware Bay every evening in the 1940s and pointed the headlights across the water at Miah Maull Light to say goodnight. One flash, four, then three meant "I LOVE YOU."

An advantage of a waterbound light was that less work was required, since there was less space to care for and no grounds to keep groomed. At Orient Point in Long Island Sound, a 1940s keeper quipped that he had no grass to mow or cows to milk, but he missed playing golf. A ball with a string attached provided hours of tee-off entertainment. For exercise, he jogged around and around the deck, calculating that one hundred circuits equaled about a mile. Similarly, Ruth Carr roller-skated on the concrete deck around Little Gull Island Lighthouse where her father worked in the 1920s. A few miles farther east in Long Island Sound, Latimer Reef's lightkeeper found time to paint beautiful seascapes on the curved interior walls and loudly played his musical instruments, knowing no one would call to complain.

James T. Somers, the last civilian keeper of Maryland's eleven-acre Cove Point Lighthouse, actually preferred offshore assignments to land stations, citing the wide variety of chores absent on waterbound towers. Isolation suited some—those who shunned society and were content with their own company. The reclusive sites also sheltered lightkeepers from colds, flu, and other contagions. One lightkeeper, retiring from work on the Chesapeake after many years, said his good health was due to the fact that "doctors could not get at me."

The drawback of offshore lighthouses was cramped space. Round walls demanded clever arrangement of possessions, and there was no place to escape loud snoring or a disagreeable coworker. At Craighill Channel Range Light near Baltimore, one keeper remarked: "It's so small, every time you sneeze you have to swab the place." Some made the most of the limited space. At Seven Foot Knoll, a screwpile lighthouse off Baltimore, the keepers constructed a wooden pen on a platform in the open framework under the tower and kept livestock in it. Window-box vegetable gardens adorned the gallery at Sandy Point Shoal in the Chesapeake Bay, and laundry sometimes flapped from a line strung between the boat davits. The cantilevered outhouse hung off the gallery, its holes open to the water below. Sometimes it was the only place to find privacy, though a cold, windy day could hamper nature's calling.

Lightkeepers' homes were usually spartan, comfortable, and clean. Regular inspections necessitated neatness and basic furnishings, as did a lifestyle supported by low pay. But expensive instruments, such as a mariner's telescope for scanning the sea, were important in the job.

Large stations like Cove Point Lighthouse near the mouth of the Patuxent River, Maryland, were demanding assignments. Unlike waterbound lighthouses, those ashore required enormous work to maintain. Grounds had to be kept groomed, and the many buildings required gallons of paint. Since there was space for a garden and livestock, land lights were allotted fewer provisions. The families spent much of their time doing farm-type chores.

Life on Miah Maull Light in the Delaware Bay was monotonous in 1946, when a Coast Guard tender snapped this photo before docking. Two keepers on the weather deck smile at its approach. Visitors, even those from the routine supply ship, were a treat. To combat their boredom, the men played cards, read books, fished, whittled, and made ships in bottles. A few learned the culinary arts. It was not unusual for a passing ship to smell the aromas of bread, chowder, or an apple pie wafting from the lighthouse kitchen. (Photograph courtesy of the United States Coast Guard)

Tedium Punctuated with Excitement

The wickies—so named because they tended simple oil lamps—had different daily tasks than their successors in the age of mechanized lighting. Wickie days were occupied with carrying oil to the lantern, cleaning and polishing the chimneys (lamp globes) and reflectors, trimming wicks, and doing general cleaning of the lantern inside and out. By 1820, they were required to keep logbooks and daily records of oil and wicks consumed, as well as file quarterly reports about their stations. Fogbells also came into use at this time, and the keepers were required to ring them by hand. Later, striking mechanisms ended the tiresome chore, but the steam signals of the 1860s created hours of work when their boilers had to be fired. Fresnel lenses, introduced in the 1840s, humbled many a lightkeeper with hundreds of delicate prisms and brass frames that demanded polish. The clockworks mechanism was brass, too, as were oilcans, fixtures on windows and doors, railings, and dustpans. The Lighthouse Board was so infatuated with this golden alloy, even the buttons on the lightkeepers' uniforms were brass.

Upkeep of buildings was a never-ending task. Salt, sand, and moisture constantly assaulted all surfaces. Towers had to be whitewashed yearly at some stations. Paint protected the ironwork, masonry, and wood. There were elaborate painted daymarks to maintain. William Collins, keeper of Assateague Light in the 1920s, built a homemade scaffold, which he pulled up and down the exterior of the tower to replenish its handsome red and white stripes. W. H. McDorman of Great Shoals Lighthouse at the entrance to the Wicomico River on the eastern shore of the Chesapeake Bay summed up the endless work in his logbook:

22 Dec: Finished painting boat . . .
2 Jan: Painted pilings down to low water . . .
3 Jan: Still painting and I am very tired . . .
9 Jan: Fixed and painted tank in storage room . . .
13 Jan: Painting floor timbers . . .
19 Jan: Painted kitchen one coat . . .

Second jobs were common early on, as keepers often had difficulty surviving on low pay. Colonial lightkeepers

Offshore lightkeepers were forced to improvise in order to make the best of cramped space. Vegetables were grown in window boxes at Sandy Point Shoal Lighthouse near Annapolis (left). Laundry was hung on a line strung over the boat davits and a small chicken coop sat on the deck. The privy of Fourteen Foot Bank Lighthouse in the Delaware Bay sat on the deck (above). Its hole opened to the water, a small porthole provided some light for occupants, and a lightning rod assured protection from heaven's wrath.

earned an average $200 a year. In 1850, a head keeper at a major station earned about $400 and his assistant $250. By the 1860s, the pay had risen to $600 and $400 respectively.

Work such as farming, fishing, piloting, ice harvesting, and lumbering augmented the family income. A few entrepreneurs operated stores and sideline businesses. Keeper Jeth Bayles opened a tavern in his quarters at Throgs Neck Lighthouse in the 1830s and boarded duck hunters. After 1852, such ventures were forbidden, but clandestine sources of income existed. Rumrunners often paid lightkeepers to turn their heads or hide the brew. Theft of government property was another way to earn a few dollars. William Wood, keeper of Point Lookout Light from 1847 to 1849, was suspected of selling government supplies on the side. When fifty-six gallons of oil were discovered missing, Wood claimed his cat fell into the supply and spoiled it. More than twenty-five replacement panes of glass also were gone, and Wood said that he had accidentally broken them. No absolute evidence of embezzlement was found, but Wood was disciplined with a reduction in pay.

With so much to do there was still boredom for some, especially at small stations where there was less work. Melinda Rose, daughter of the lightkeeper at Stony Point along the Hudson River in the 1890s, apathetically noted: "I can't remember anything that has ever happened, except once our cow died, and several times it's been bad for the chickens." Another keeper, perhaps to underscore the ennui, humorously penned in his logbook: "Killed a mosquito today." Hobbies were a rare indulgence until the modern era when conveniences and better pay freed up the keeper to pursue leisure activities. At Fishing Battery Light one man carved decoys; another at Turkey Point did crossword puzzles. Harry Palmer, keeper at Cape May in the 1920s, won blue ribbons at the city flower show for his prize hydrangeas.

Many lightkeepers were ardent readers, encouraged by the introduction of circulating libraries in 1877. The U.S. Lighthouse Board had special wooden bookcases made with doors and a handle for transporting books. About fifty titles were included in each case, mostly classic novels and subjects intended to engender "moral thought." The tenders exchanged libraries every few months when supplies were delivered. In its 1885 annual report the Lighthouse Board stated that some seven hundred libraries were in circulation and "preference is given to their distribution to those light stations most distant from towns and villages." By the twentieth century, the project was overseen by the Merchant Marine Association, and all books and magazines were donated.

A Plethora of Perils

Each season brought unique challenges for the lighthouse keeper. Ice and snow cloaked the lantern in winter, obscuring the light, and extra hours of darkness meant longer watches. Lard oil, used in many lighthouses, had to be heated in the house then hurriedly taken to the lamps and poured before it congealed. Fuel supplies quickly ran out in the coldest years or were limited by wartime economy. "On account of no coal this winter," wrote Hog Island lightkeeper C. A. Sterling in 1918, "I have collected driftwood from the river enough to run me through winter." The same year, Cold Spring Lighthouse on Long Island suffered significant damage from ice grinding against the tower. Keeper Louis P. Brown reported doors being pushed open, dishes falling out of cupboards, and a great vibration that extinguished the beacon and caused the lighthouse to "sway, crack, and tremble." The keeper of Greenbury Point Shoal Lighthouse near Annapolis radioed his superiors: "You are respectfully informed that at 1 o'clock this morning the ice broke adrift; at 1:30 A.M. the lamp in the lens upset and was put out of commission, and a minute later the lens fell off the pedestal and broke all to pieces, together with storm panes. . . . Everything in the house was upset except the stove and water tanks."

The winter of 1936 brought a pounding nor'easter to Long Island. The Cornfield Point Lightship reported 70 mph winds and high seas that left the vessel with a coating of ice from four to fifteen inches thick. Nearby, waterbound Race Rock Lighthouse suffered as well. "I could not get down on the dock, as the seas were breaking on the main deck," the keeper wrote. "The boat was covered with ice from 8 to 10 inches on top of the cover, and from 18 to 20 inches on the stern. I and the first assistant worked all day of the 25th and 26th chopping out the boat and getting ice out of the stern off the engine box."

Even in the modern era of lightkeeping, winter plagued the lights. Coast Guard keepers at Ship John Shoal Light in the Delaware Bay weathered the ice storm of 1961 with good cheer, despite many hardships. Hank

Above: *Prior to electrification, lighthouses were more vulnerable to fire due to the flammable illuminants used in the lamps. Mineral oil, in particular, was a volatile fuel. When it was approved for use in lighthouses in the 1870s, the U.S. Lighthouse Board began building detached oilhouses to store it. The simple oil shed at Turkey Point Lighthouse served this purpose until 1944 when the station was electrified.*

Facing page: *Next to caring for the beacon, painting occupied most of the keeper's time. Elaborate daymarks, like this one at Virginia's Assateague Lighthouse, had to be maintained to distinguish the towers from their surroundings. A variety of contrivances assisted in the repainting. When a ladder exhausted its reach, makeshift scaffolds took over, or a chair fastened with ropes and pulleys was slung over the side. It wasn't a job for acrophobics.*

Lindemann was worried when food supplies and drinking water ran low, and the tower became a prison of sorts: "The door coming in the north side was completely frozen shut. Our only way in and out was through the galley or engine room windows. Even the fog signal froze up. We did get it operating using hot water but it still kept freezing up." Lindemann radioed Cape May for help. After several days, a tender was able to safely make a landing, free the frozen door, and replenish supplies.

If not ice, then a ship might collide with a lighthouse. Catherine Murdock, keeper at Roundout Light from 1867 to 1907, looked up from her sewing one morning to see the bowsprit of a Hudson River schooner crash through a window. The vessel had been forced too close to the lighthouse by a string of towed barges. Similarly, a schooner hit Tangier Sound Light in 1905 after ice pushed it too near the tower. Four years later, Thimble

Shoal Light was slammed by a schooner, upsetting the stove and starting a fire that completely destroyed the lighthouse. The two keepers barely escaped in the station boat. Collisions continue to cripple lighthouses today. The huge Texas tower lighthouse at Ambrose, New York, was rammed by a tanker in 1996 and irreparably damaged.

In summer, lightning sought the skyscraping cupolas and metal parts of lighthouses. Cape Henlopen Light lost its cornice to a bolt from the blue in 1872. Sandy Hook Light has been struck at least a dozen times. Storms sent keepers scrambling to the roof to scrub away dirt and bird droppings so that clean rainwater could fill the cisterns. Hail shattered windows, and heavy rains flooded river and backwater lights. Moths swarmed around the beacons, fouling the oil and leaving a fine dust on the lamps and lenses. In spring and fall, birds traveling the Great Atlantic Flyway passed by, sometimes with disastrous results. Late summer and early fall also brought the peak of the hurricane season.

In 1933, John J. Daley endured an August hurricane at Drum Point Lighthouse with fifteen-foot seas slamming the little tower and flooding its rooms. The keeper's boat was ripped from its davits and the screwpile legs were pounded with debris, including a large tree that lodged against the base. Daley "made every effort to save Station property but wind, tide, and sea were against" him. He was marooned on the lighthouse for several days with no way to get ashore. During the same storm, York Spit lightkeeper W. J. Diggs wrote: "Floors began to burst up. Sailboat broke away. Sea breaking over deck. Oil tanks broke away." A passing fishing boat rescued him from the reeling lighthouse.

The infamous September 1938 hurricane slammed lighthouses in the Long Island area and tossed the tender *Tulip* onto railroad tracks next to her berth as if she were a toy boat. Oil and water tanks were torn off the deck at Race Rock Light and seawater inundated the first floor. At Latimer Reef Lighthouse George Durfee scrambled to rescue his belongings, including a beautiful model of the lighthouse he had made, when the storm surged through the bottom of the tower. His compatriot, Frank Jo Raymond, was more adventuresome, rushing outside at the height of the storm to take pictures. These were later made into postcards and sold in area stores for twenty-five cents each.

As if seasonal catastrophes weren't enough, nature cooked up unexpected histrionics. On August 31, 1886, Herman Dehl reported a vibration in the tower at

Thick, lustrous prisms in the lens at Sandy Hook Lighthouse break light into a cascade of rainbows over the brass framework. Introduced to lighthouses in the United States in the 1840s, prismatic lenses vastly improved the range and clarity of lights and introduced flashing characteristics. Lightkeepers reacted ambivalently—glad for a superior apparatus but dismayed at the amount of work required to maintain it.

Maryland's Cove Point Light that lasted only a few seconds. A rare earthquake centered near Charleston, South Carolina, had been felt as far north as New York. The tremors sent cracks up the walls of the old Cape Henry Light and were recorded at a number of other lighthouses. The U.S. Geological Service interviewed lightkeepers throughout the Mid-Atlantic and South to gather important data on the event.

Even the most unexpected perils existed. Four men aboard Holland Island Bar Lighthouse in 1957 thought a war had broken out on the Chesapeake Bay when U.S.

Diminutive Stony Point Lighthouse was the first sentinel to guide shipping on the Hudson River north of New York City. Its panoramic view and farm-field surroundings made it a pleasant assignment, albeit somewhat lonely and lackluster compared to coastal lighthouses. Nancy Rose took over as keeper in 1856 following the death of her husband and served for forty-eight years, most of them without incident. To bide her time when not tending the lamps, she polished the copper floor of the lantern and scrubbed the interior walls. After the area was declared a state park in honor of a 1779 Revolutionary War battle, Rose found a new pastime giving tours of the lighthouse and recounting how her great-grandfather had been wounded helping General "Mad" Anthony Wayne defeat the British.

Simple furnishings with a Victorian touch served Keeper Freeling Hewitt and his family at Hereford Inlet Lighthouse in the 1880s. Freeling's wife and daughters spent much of their leisure time doing needlework, as reflected in the fine lace covers for the bed, pillows, and washstand.

WHEN LADIES LIT THE LAMPS

A mighty woman with a torch, whose flame
Is the imprisoned lightning.
Emma Lazarus, "The New Colossus," 1883

The traditional image of the lightkeeper is decidedly masculine; yet official records show that hundreds of women worked as lightkeepers, beginning in the colonial era when Hannah Thomas assumed care of the Plymouth light in Massachusetts after her husband died in the Revolutionary War. Women worked as paid assistants to their husbands, fathers, and brothers, or were appointed outright as head keepers at small stations. "Lighthouse Widows" were the norm, for seldom could a woman be hired had she not served an apprentice-type tenure under a man, namely her husband.

Maryland lighthouses seemed to attract the ladies. At Piney Point Lighthouse three women served between 1850 and 1900. Josephine Wilson kept Blackstone Island Light for thirty-six years, beginning in 1876, and Martha and Pamelia Edwards—mother and daughter—worked at Point Lookout Light from 1854 to 1869. But it was Turkey Point Light at the tip of Elk Neck where ladies had the longest careers. Elizabeth Lusby served from 1844 to 1861, and Rebecca Crouch from 1873 to 1895, followed by her daughter Georgiana Crouch Brumfield until 1919. It was then that the devoted career of Fanny Salter began, drawing public acclaim for the ladies of the lamps.

Mrs. Salter assisted her husband, Harry Salter, with his work at the lighthouse. When he died in 1925, she asked to continue as lightkeeper but was denied presumably because of her age and the remoteness of the station. Mrs. Salter wrote to her congressman, who in turn appealed to President Calvin Coolidge. He approved her request, possibly because the station still operated with oil lamps and did not require heavy work or mechanical knowledge. At age forty-two, Fanny Salter became the last civilian woman appointed to the Lighthouse Service. Her career as head keeper spanned twenty-two years and earned her a special place in Chesapeake Bay history.

Life at Turkey Point was peaceful and fulfilling, though challenged by a lack of modern conveniences. The house was lighted with oil lamps and heated by a woodstove. It wasn't until 1944 that electricity and a radiotelephone set were installed. An automatic fogbell striker had been added not long after Mrs. Salter's appointment, but it sometimes failed, and she was forced to ring the bell by hand. Winter snows frequently closed the access road to the lighthouse, sequestering her on the point. She had no complaints, however. Solitude and a simple life suited her.

The lighthouse tender *Maple* delivered wood, coal, and other supplies and took care of repairs. In addition, Keeper Salter kept watch on the various buoys and channel lights in her area and reported any problems to the tender. She raised chickens, sheep, and turkeys, gardened, canned, sewed, read, and did puzzles. "I never seem to get enough of crossword puzzles," she once told a reporter. "My friends send me hundreds, but I'm always fresh out." For company and protection, she kept a Chesapeake Bay retriever.

Shortly before her retirement in 1947, the Coast Guard authorized a publicity photo shoot at Turkey Point. Fanny Salter was pictured wearing a suit and dress shoes, her gray hair tucked in a bun and spectacles perched on her nose, lovingly tending the new electric light. She left the station at age sixty-four and moved to a home only six miles away where she could see the lighthouse flashing each night.

Today all that remains of the station—tended so much of its career by feminine hands—is the old masonry tower.

Greenbury Point near Annapolis, Maryland, saw a succession of calamities. After shoals built up off the mouth of the Severn River, erosion rendered useless its first lighthouse, built in 1849. The cottage-style sentinel was torn down and replaced in 1891 by a screwpile tower standing on the shoals. It, too, succumbed when heavy ice buildup in the winter of 1918 crushed it. (Photograph courtesy of the United States Coast Guard)

Navy fighter planes mistook the lighthouse for an intended practice target and fired three rockets into its walls. The same lighthouse had been the subject of a great mystery years earlier, when keeper Ulman Owens was found dead in his bedroom. His body lay near a bloody knife, and there was evidence of a struggle. Investigators blamed the murder on rumrunners.

Fire was one of the worst dangers for lightkeepers, and wood its principal victim. Wooden decks and stairways were vulnerable, as were the many wooden outbuildings. At some sites, the entire station was constructed of wood. Waterbound lightkeepers were the most defenseless, for once kindled their towers were like ships aflame at sea. Fires were usually caused by combustible fuels and human error. In 1960, a spark set off a small

fire in the compressor room at Bloody Point Bar Light in the Chesapeake Bay. Two young Coast Guard keepers battled the blaze for several minutes with extinguishers as it spread through their quarters and raged toward the storage room where a five-hundred-gallon gas tank was kept. Realizing the danger, they dove for the powerboat hanging in its davits and hit the water running. Moments later, an explosion rocked the lighthouse and flames shot high into the night sky. The tower's metal exterior glowed red hot as its wooden lining burned. Only a shell remained the next day.

Lighthouse life wasn't all strife and misfortune. For some, it was a calling and a labor of love. James T. Bolling was so enamored of the lighthouse at Seven Foot Knoll that when his daughter was born in the tower in June

The reclusive assignment at Bloody Point Bar Lighthouse, near Kent Island in Chesapeake Bay, was tedious and lonely. Dampness crept into the pantry and bunks, making for soggy sleeping, and winter cold was almost unbearable. Yearly ice floes grinding against the tower had pushed it five degrees out of vertical—enough to send coffee cups sliding across the kitchen table on a windy day. When a fire broke out in April 1960 and the two keepers on duty barely escaped with their lives, the Coast Guard closed up the tower for good and automated the beacon.

1875 he named her "Knollie." Benjamin Porter Greenwood was keeper of Jones Point Light for thirty-seven years; he raised fourteen children on the little Potomac River station and died in 1903 while tending the beacon.

Logbooks, normally terse and business-like, occasionally mentioned glorious tangerine sunsets, eclipses of the moon, or the tatted veil of snowflakes swirling through the tower's effulgent beams. Stephen Jones poignantly wrote of a 1961 snowstorm that expunged his littoral world of its usual grayness and left Harbor of Refuge Light looking like a frosted wedding cake: "It was along some parts of the rail, in patches on the balcony deck, in the corners of the windows, and—the great marvel—down the breakwater . . . real snow lying deep but light, so that all the cracks were filled and on the landing stage was a puffy quilt."

Less Than Noble

Not everyone who applied for lighthouse work was suited for the job. Between 1885 and 1889, nearly 1,200 new lightkeepers were hired. More than half resigned, most within five years. Isolation, boredom, the monotony of the work, low pay, and long hours standing watch forced many out of the service. More frequent than resignations were dismissals. Absence from duty and sleeping on watch were common reasons for termination, but drunkenness was at the top of the list. Grace Humes of Long Island remembered climbing to the lantern of Fire

Island Lighthouse around 1910 with her grandmother, wife of the absent head keeper, and finding one of his assistants "passed out drunk" on the lantern floor. The women tended the light until the head keeper returned.

The attrition rate at some stations was surprising. Brandywine Shoal Light lost four keepers in a single decade; two more were dismissed for dereliction duty and another two drowned. Eber Hudson appears to have been content on the lonely tower, however. He came aboard in 1872 as a third assistant, earning four hundred dollars annually. By 1893, he had risen in rank to become head keeper at a salary of seven hundred dollars. Compare his tenacious duty to the temporal career of John Sheen who was appointed to Schuykill River Lighthouse near Philadelphia in mid December 1875 and resigned before New Year's Day.

Indolence was tempting in the early years, as there were few rules to abide by and seldom did the collectors of customs check on work or the conditions at a lighthouse. Complaints by local residents often were considered vindictive and inflated—ploys to have a keeper ousted so that his job might become available. Protests from shipmasters seemed to garner greater response, and then only a mild rebuke from the administration. Piney Point's lightkeeper in the 1830s frequently left the station in the hands of his black slave woman and her son and was found missing on the very day an inspector paid a surprise visit in 1841. Women weren't immune from censure either. Charlotte Suter, also of Piney Point Light,

Many mid-Atlantic lighthouses stand watch along the Great Atlantic Flyway. Avian traffic during the migration periods of autumn and spring poses a danger to the towers, as birds are mysteriously drawn to the lights and dash themselves against walls and windows.

was dismissed in 1846 for neglecting the light in order to spend more time in the tavern she operated nearby.

Cape Henry Lighthouse suffered a stretch of incompetence in the early 1870s. District Inspector W. F. Stanley repeatedly found the station in a dirty, disheveled condition. Head keeper Henry Richardson complained bitterly that his two assistants left without permission and did not attend to their duties. But when the two were replaced, the situation did not improve. Richardson was discharged in 1874, and his replacement, Horatio Creekman, put the station in order. His successor unfortunately fell back to slovenly habits. The logbook for March 16, 1880, read: "Mr. Brown, the former keeper, moved away leaving the house in bad order. We cleaned over two cart loads of sand and dirt out of his kitchen."

The station logbook for Navesink Twin Lights noted on August 28, 1877: "Schenck Waling, 2nd asst. and Charles Murphy, 3rd asst. were discharged from this station. They were both charged for insubordination and bad conduct generally." A few years later on June 19, 1881, the logbook read: "2nd asst. was intoxicated and not fit for duty; sent a report to the inspector about the disgrace of his conduct." The next day the second assistant's resignation was noted. There was concern for the mariner, of course, but also a public image to uphold. Like the town minister or the local sheriff, the lightkeeper bore the burden of an entirely righteous character, whether he possessed one or not.

Life in a Fishbowl

Publicity was part of the job, especially at land lights. The public was enamored of lightkeepers, and the keepers, for the most part, enjoyed the adulation. Vacation days were granted, but limited, and required advance approval. Thus, there was little time off or chance to socialize outside the station. Visitors were sometimes the only contact a lighthouse family had with the greater world. They came in buggies on Sundays to tour the lighthouse, play on the beach, and picnic on its grounds, or they arrived by boat, often bearing gifts for the keeper—a jar of jam, a smoked ham, books, or a bottle of rum, though alcohol at lighthouses was forbidden. Also prohibited was the boarding of visitors. When the keeper lit up for the night, his company had to be gone.

The resort lights at places like Fire Island, Barnegat Inlet, Cape May, Cape Henlopen, and Cape Henry were never short on visitors in summer. Absecon Light was one of the most popular, reporting 10,339 visitors in 1912 and nearly double that number by 1930. At Cape May in the late nineteenth century, seaside vacationers rode buggies on the hard-packed sand to reach the lighthouse. By 1900, they could ride the beach trolley and stop at the lighthouse to buy tomatoes from the garden or bait boxes made by the assistant keeper, Ed Hughes. A few years later, keeper Harry Palmer received the Bureau of Lighthouses' award for "best kept lawn," an impressive honor considering the number of guests trampling the grass each year. At Old Point Comfort Lighthouse in Hampton Roads, so many visitors came in the 1920s the government supplied sixty-three assorted plants, eight packs of flower seeds, a lawnmower, and a garden hose— all to keep the grounds pretty.

Official instructions to keepers advised that they "must be courteous and polite to visitors and show them everything of interest about the station at such times as will not interfere with light-house duties. Keepers must not allow visitors to handle the apparatus or deface light-house property. Special care must be taken to prevent the scratching of names or initials on the glass of the lanterns or on the windows of the towers."

Thomas Buckridge, keeper of Montauk Point Light in the 1920s, had to keep the station privies locked so that tourists would not use them. His lighthouse was open to the public every day except Sunday. His daughter, Margaret Bock, recalls: "It was the responsibility of the keeper on watch to walk up and down the stairs with each group of visitors. Often, in the summer, when there were thousands of visitors, one man would be stationed at the foot of the tower and one in the lantern, letting visitors up at intervals. Sometimes the visitors were fun and broke the monotony of our semi-isolation. At other times they were obnoxious. Some of them tried to rip the shingles off the house for souvenirs."

At lonely Fenwick Island Lighthouse prior to the development of Ocean City, the keepers had an unusual visitor on Christmas Day in 1932. An Eskimo was found on the beach, exhausted from a long journey south from Greenland. He was taken in, warmed and fed, and small repairs were made to his canoe. He claimed to be headed to the Panama Canal. The reason for the trip was never revealed. The keepers were so amazed by his story that they reported the visit to the Bureau, and the tale appeared in the U.S. *Lighthouse Service Bulletin.*

Victorian-era journalists saw lighthouses and their keepers as subjects of great dramas. Gustav Kobbe, writ-

IN THE PATH OF GREAT MIGRATIONS

I wanted to spend a night in a lighthouse when the birds were flying; to see the small travelers pouring out of the darkness into the dazzling beams.
Roger Tory Peterson

The Great Atlantic Flyway is the Eastern Seaboard's feathered freeway, a busy migration route that passes a number of lighthouses. In spring and autumn, lighthouse keepers witnessed thousands of birds winging overhead during daylight hours, but at dusk the weary avians became easily confused, even blinded, by the bright beams of light. The outcome was often tragic.

Cape Henry's second lighthouse had barely baptized its logbook with ink when the keeper recorded on May 8, 1883: "Hundreds of small birds killed last night by striking the tower and lantern." A century later, Coast Guard keepers were still reporting damage from birds. At Fourteen Foot Bank Light, deep in the Delaware Bay, Ray Pfaff heard a loud crash one cold night in 1964. He dropped his coffee cup and raced to the lantern. Broken glass littered the deck, along with a dead seagull that had somehow lost its way in 55 mph winds. The collision destroyed the tower's important red sector panel that warned ships of the shallows nearby.

Lightkeepers at Fishing Battery Lighthouse, surrounded by islands of grass in the Susquehanna Flats of the northern Chesapeake Bay, estimated as many as 800,000 ducks and geese passed near their tower between October and December. Hunters boasted of bagging hundreds a season. The fowl provided many meals for the lightkeepers, but they also sometimes created additional work, as keepers had to clean up when they flew into the lantern.

At Shinnecock Lighthouse on Long Island, wintering Canada geese caused damage to the lantern windows and expensive lens. Chicken wire was wrapped around the lantern, but geese still pelted it, their large bodies snagging in the wire screen. So many were killed that lightkeepers dug a trench around the lighthouse to dispose of them. When hunters heard about the glut of birds, they swarmed the island. The government declared the area a wildlife refuge to protect the lightkeepers and the precious lens from gunfire.

A more serious problem occurred at Virginia's Hog Island Lighthouse in February 1900. A bitter northwest cold front pushed flocks toward warmer air over the coast and produced a sort of avian traffic jam. Keepers were surprised when hundreds of birds, large and small, began striking the tower just after sunset one evening. By midnight the lantern glass was broken and the beacon extinguished. The men fired shots in the air in an attempt to frighten the birds, to no avail. With ammunition gone, they retreated to the base of the tower. Near dawn the feathered raiders gave up their assault. A grisly scene greeted the men when they stepped outside—more than a hundred dead brants, ducks, geese, and smaller songbirds.

Facing page and above: *Birds were both a boon and a bane at lighthouses. Many keepers were avid birdwatchers, and the fowl often provided table fare when little else was available, but collisions with the lantern proved costly.*

Not all encounters were so fatal. Many lightkeepers enjoyed birdwatching, and the wilderness milieu in which they worked provided ample specimens to observe. Lightkeeper Charles A. Sterling, who came to Hog Island Light in 1903, loved the birds he saw winging through the beams:

"The brandt, the shyest, wildest, most timid of the waterfowl, were within five feet of us, but evidently blinded by the light, they could see nothing. Some would circle around the tower, others dart by; and wonderful to relate, some would remain stationary in the air, their wings moving so rapidly that they were blurred like a wheel in rapid motion. I thought at the time what a tremendous power must lie in their wings to enable them to nullify the wind."

Even the smallest sentinels were important to navigation. For over a century, little Jones Point Lighthouse warned of sandbars in the Potomac River. For much of that time it was in the capable care of Benjamin Porter Greenwood who regarded his work as a calling. He and his wife raised fourteen children at the lighthouse, and Greenwood died while on duty in 1903.

Storm clouds threaten Cove Point Lighthouse. The lightning rod on its cupola is a reminder of the vulnerability of lofty towers.

ing for *Century Magazine* in the 1890s, enticed visitors with biblical metaphors and descriptions of breathtaking ocean vistas: "Rising with an antique grace from among their picturesque environs, they seem peculiarly fitted to shed their light like a benediction upon the waves." Engravings accentuated the seaside setting and made lighthouses adventurous destinations. The twentieth century further transformed lighthouses into media icons. The lonely lightkeeper became a nostalgic symbol of hard work and family values and his light an instrument of goodwill. Hudson-Athens lightkeeper, Emil Brunner, was pictured on the December 1946 cover of the *Saturday Evening Post* rowing home to the lighthouse in a snowfall with his children and a Christmas tree in the boat.

Christmas was when the lightkeepers received the warmest publicity. Newspaper reporters caught neighbors delivering gifts and food to lighthouses. Throughout the first half of the twentieth century, the Seaman's Church Institute sent warm knitted hats and gloves, and in the 1940s, Mrs. Edward Harkness, a rich widow from Connecticut, saw that every lightkeeper in Long Island Sound had a radio. The Flying Santa of the Lighthouses, a.k.a. Edward Rowe Snow, traveled the East Coast from 1937 to 1982 with parcels of presents for the keepers. These were dropped from a small plane in what Snow termed a "Christmas Bombing." His pilot flew close to a lighthouse, and when the angle was right, the package was flung from the plane. With luck, it landed on the lawn or snagged on the tower. Inside was an assortment

Golden evening light washes the windows and doors of the keeper's quarters at Montauk Point Lighthouse.

of goodies—candy, gum, razor blades, cigarettes, calendars, and cookies reduced to crumbs by the impact. Snow always included one of his books, too, usually *Famous Lighthouses of America*.

There were times when Christmas was not so cheerful. The Newport News *Daily Press* reported a sorrowful day at Newport News Middle Ground Lighthouse on December 24, 1938. William Brown, a relief keeper on the light, had gone ashore early in the day to buy the holiday meal for himself and the head keeper, Captain A. L. Cox. He'd also picked up the mail and some gifts for his comrade. As he rowed back to the lighthouse late on Christmas Eve, "freezing spray forming a rimey coat of ice over his oilskins," he saw the silhouette of Cox on the deck, waiting for him. As he drew beneath the caisson on which the lighthouse perched, a line dropped down, and he made the boat fast. A hand reached out in the darkness to help. The heavy bundle was handed up, then Brown struggled to the deck with a shout of "Merry Christmas!" There was no answer. Captain Cox lay on the planking next to the bundle. His heart had failed.

Fanning upwards, the spiral staircase at Cove Point Lighthouse echoes with the footsteps of many lightkeepers. Now part of Calvert Marine Museum, it invites visitors to climb to the top for a bird's-eye view of the Chesapeake Bay.

Economy of space and a lack of square walls forced families at some lighthouses to find creative room arrangements, such as tucking beds into window dormers.

Lighthouses have long been considered interesting places to visit. Old Point Comfort Light at Fort Monroe, Virginia, was so popular with tourists and dignitaries in the 1920s its keepers had an allotment of plants and tools for landscaping. Its grounds are kept well groomed even today.

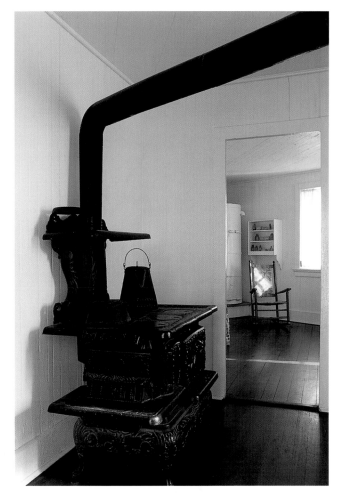

Mealtime was the highlight of the day on waterbound tow-ers. The table at Hooper Strait Lighthouse probably over-looked the busy channel through Tangier Sound. Hot coffee was always kept ready in case someone stopped by, but at such a lonely site there was little chance for visitors.

The pipe of the cast-iron stove at Hooper Strait Lighthouse snakes its way up to the ceiling and out through the roof. The fire rarely was allowed to go out, for it was the only source of heat. Winters on the Chesapeake Bay were bitter, a time when the kitchen stove became a family friend.

Stories such as these pepper the pages of lighthouse history. But they are just that—history. The traditional lightkeeper lives on only in memory, a beloved person-ality who grows more endearing and legendary with pass-ing years. Flesh and breath have gone out of the work, replaced by mechanical gadgets and electronic wizardry. Still, something vital lives on. The lightkeeper of the twenty-first century wears a new identity.

CHAPTER 6

The New Keepers

Left: *Deactivated in 1954 and a target for vandals, Hooper Strait Lighthouse was adopted by the Chesapeake Bay Maritime Museum. Disassembled on site and moved piece by piece forty miles upriver to the museum grounds in 1966, it now has a new career educating the public.*

Above: *Saving the material culture of lighthouses includes preservation of the ancillary buildings associated with each site. The fogbell tower from Point Lookout Lighthouse was moved to Chesapeake Bay Maritime Museum years ago to ensure its proper care and interpretation. Bell towers were designed to hold the mechanism that struck the bell. Tower height allowed sound to travel over the water and made space for the weights to drop from the clockworks system of the striker.*

A light without a keeper is but half a light.
Horace Beck, *Folklore and the Sea*, 1973

"Lighthouse Weekend" is one of New Jersey's most popular and well-attended events—a farewell to summer and a salute to New Jersey's coastal heritage rolled into one. All along the shore, the state's lighthouses open their doors to visitors. Participants are encouraged to visit eleven mainland lighthouses in two days and, if successful, they receive a certificate of commemorative stamps and recognition as members of the elite "Eleven Points of Light Club." The celebration was inaugurated in 2000 by the New Jersey Lighthouse Society, a group of more than 1,000 enthusiasts dedicated to lighthouse preservation and education.

"Something like this never would have happened twenty years ago," says Yvonne Miller, first vice president and program chair for the society. "We've seen interest increase year after year."

Miller grew up along the Delaware River and has loved lighthouses for much of her life. Surprised and pleased with the recent upsurge in interest in lighthouses, she sees important work ahead for groups like hers. The towers need work, the artifacts should be saved and displayed, and the story of the lightkeeping era begs to be told. Nearly all of New Jersey's lighthouses have sponsoring organizations to care for them. These groups are part of a larger regional network that gathers annually at Calvert Marine Museum in the Chesapeake Bay to share information and develop better outreach programs. A common goal is education. Getting the public to visit the lighthouses is where it begins.

Tim Harrison, president of the American Lighthouse Foundation, believes lighthouse preservation sells itself: "Once people see the lighthouses and realize how special they are—their beauty, the stories of the keepers, how much history is packed into each one—then they want to get involved. We've already lost too many lighthouses. We've got to try to save the rest."

Harrison publishes a "Doomsday List" of lighthouses in danger of being lost and has been surprisingly successful in raising awareness, as well as funding, for restoration. When Mispillion Lighthouse appeared on the list in the late 1990s, the Delaware communities of Milford and Slaughter Beach rallied with monetary contributions and offers to help refurbish it. The ramshackle 1873 sentinel was deactivated in 1921 and had been sold at auction. Over the years, its keeper's house with attached square tower—the last wooden lighthouse on the

Hereford Inlet Lighthouse is one of eleven mainland sentinels featured during Lighthouse Weekend in New Jersey. Travelers hope to visit all "Eleven Points of Light" to learn something of the Garden State's history and earn a special certificate from the New Jersey Lighthouse Society.

Delaware Bay and one of the oldest in the state—has deteriorated badly. Fire and vandalism are concerns, and erosion brings the bay closer to the foundation with every storm. The Keepers of Mispillion Light, incorporated in 2000, are determined to rescue the lighthouse.

Small, nonprofit groups like this one are the mainstays of lighthouse preservation. About half of all the lighthouses still standing in the Mid-Atlantic are cared for in this way. Members of preservation groups are passionate and energetic, often with some personal connection to a particular lighthouse. Jim Milsted, a volunteer with the Tinicum Rear Range Lighthouse Society, grew up in the shadow of the eighty-five-foot iron tower and remembers bringing sandwiches to the Coast Guard crews sent out to paint it. Tony Tuliano, a former Coast Guard keeper at Plum Island Light on Long Island, is active

Ramshackle Mispillion Lighthouse is one of about a dozen mid-Atlantic lighthouses included on the American Lighthouse Foundation's "Doomsday List," and with good reason. Scheduled for restoration by the Keepers of Mispillion Light when this picture was taken in 2001, it burned after being hit by lightning May 2, 2002. Most of the upper part of the tower was destroyed.

with "Save Plum Island," contributing to the group's website.

Not all organizations are young. Friends of Fenwick Island Lighthouse dates back to the late 1970s when the Coast Guard deactivated the beacon, removed its keepers and the lens, and stripped it of all wiring. The lighthouse had outlived its usefulness. High-rise hotels dwarfed the tower and a glitter of city lights made it impossible for ships to find its beacon. Paul Pepper, grandson of the light's last keeper, feared it might be torn down. His letter-writing campaign reached across the bay to Washington, D.C., and saved the oldest standing structure in Ocean City, Delaware.

One of the first organizations to form on behalf of lighthouses was the U.S. Lighthouse Society, led by a former Coast Guard officer who could easily pass for one of yesterday's lightkeepers. Wayne Wheeler, gray-whiskered and gruff-voiced, saw the plight of abandoned and automated lighthouses. In 1984, he set out to save them, working from his kitchen table. His parent organization, which today boasts more than 11,000 members, has migrated to a San Francisco office building and given birth to a number of offspring, including chapters on Long Island and the Chesapeake Bay. These larger groups serve as clearinghouses for their regions and support numerous large-scale lighthouse preservation projects.

Rescue of the obsolete Cedar Island Lighthouse is a top priority for the Long Island Chapter of the U.S. Lighthouse Society. The group collects rare books, personal family papers, official documents, memorabilia, and artifacts, including an 1880s lighthouse service boat that's being restored for eventual public display. Restoring lighthouses is the chapter's forte. Cedar Island Light was once a beacon for the whaling community at Sag Harbor. The original wooden sentinel was built on Cedar Island in 1839. The present 1868 granite lighthouse was abandoned by the Lighthouse Service in 1934 and owned privately for many years before becoming part of a county park. The Long Island Chapter has stabilized the structure and is raising money to restore it.

Volunteers in the Chesapeake Chapter, with membership largely from Maryland and Virginia, are more focused on support. They regularly visit the Coast Guard historian's office in Washington, D.C., to maintain hundreds of lighthouse files and help process the many requests for information the office receives.

A work crew in jeans and sweatshirts also visits the Coast Guard's warehouse at Forestville, Maryland, several times a year to clean and repair historic Fresnel lenses. Volunteer Marie Vincent describes the challenges faced when working with old optics: "Repairing these lenses is like a giant jigsaw puzzle. Our first problem is to get the frames back in shape by gently warping them with clamps. Then acid-free paper is wound around the brass and strapping tape applied on top to form a band around the frame. Prisms are then fitted back into place."

The work is delicate and tedious, but gratifying. Once the lenses are cleaned and repaired, they can be given to museums for public display rather than left to gather dust in the warehouse. A database created by chapter volunteers helps identify where each lens may have served.

"I am in awe of the artisans who made these items back in the nineteenth century under what we would consider to be less than desirable conditions," Vincent says. "Their craftsmanship deserves to be appreciated, not just stored in a crate somewhere."

Vincent is among the new lighthouse keepers— volunteers who scrape paint, cut grass, clean windows, polish brass, sell t-shirts and mugs, visit schools, donate lighthouse books to libraries, hold fundraisers, and give guided tours. They attend municipal meetings to encourage community involvement and make political connections; a few have spoken before Congress. Their cars sport bumper stickers with catch phrases such as "I Brake for Lighthouses" or "Save the Lights." Dedication runs high. The Coast Guard says its mission to maintain lighthouses would be considerably more difficult without the help of such volunteer groups.

Lights and Showpieces

Though not in the business of historic restoration, the Coast Guard often finds itself deeply involved in lighthouse projects. "This isn't what we're mandated to do," points out Dr. Robert Browning, Coast Guard historian, "but lighthouses present a unique problem in that people feel so strongly about them."

The issue of what to do with obsolete and unmanned historic lighthouses actually predates the Coast Guard era, to a time when the Bureau of Lighthouses began modernizing and economizing its operations. Of the 1,500 lighthouses standing in 1920, roughly half remain. Some were torn down immediately upon retirement; others deteriorated, were vandalized, and were eventually razed. Though the public had yet to catch "lighthouse fever," a few discontinued lighthouses were transferred into community hands before World War II, but

Perhaps its resemblance to a country church is what endears Plum Island Lighthouse to a passionate group of Long Island residents, who hope to rescue it from an uncertain future. Uninhabited since 1968, the granite sentinel is one of six in Long Island Sound and New York Harbor built on the same design.

not with any particular guidelines for use. Retired lighthouses sometimes took on new roles as gift shops, restaurants, beach cottages, ice cream parlors, and adornments for golf courses, lawns, and marinas.

Sands Point became a private residence, owned by William Randolph Hearst in the 1930s. He threw lavish parties on the lighthouse lawn. Similar fates befell Dumpling Rock Light in Long Island Sound and New Dorp Light on Staten Island, both converted to private estates. Princes Bay Lighthouse was deactivated in 1922 and sold to a Catholic mission, which replaced the beacon with a statue of the Virgin Mary and converted the keeper's house into a retreat center. Few people considered that such second careers might compromise the historic integrity of lighthouses or somehow insult their structural pride.

When control of the country's lighthouses was transferred to the Coast Guard in 1939, automation stepped up, bringing with it a new set of problems with the un-

manning of many still-operative lights. Removing resident keepers left the towers and ancillary buildings vulnerable to the elements and vandalism. The issue escalated in the 1960s—a time, fortunately, when heritage-consciousness was growing and government legislation was enacted to protect historic structures. Lighthouses especially benefited. Towers were turned over to the General Services Administration, which sought appropriate uses for lighthouses—uses that preserved historic value and optimized public benefit. Lighthouses were included in the Historic American Buildings Survey, and many were admitted to national and state registers of historic places; as a result, they were absorbed by museums, state and national parks, and a variety of private preservation groups.

The ordeal of functional obsolescence and subsequent revitalization as a public landmark was played out time and again. In 1970, the Coast Guard decided to demolish Orient Point Lighthouse, a little caisson tower in Long Island Sound that had leaned five degrees out of plumb due to foundation problems. Public opposition to loss of the "CoffeePot," as the little beacon was affectionately nicknamed, was enormous. The Coast Guard was flummoxed. What appeal was there in such a homely hunk of metal? Plenty, as it turned out. Ferries laden with tourists passed by it, fishermen and recreational boaters loved it, and gift shops hawked postcards and calendars bearing its quaint image. The government reconsidered; in 1973, restoration of the little beacon began with a coat of special epoxy paint to maintain its exterior. Still slightly canted, Orient Point Lighthouse celebrated its centennial in 1999, with a giant banner draped around her middle like a girl in a beauty pageant.

The defunct screwpile lighthouses at Drum Point, Hooper Strait, and Seven Foot Knoll were lifted off their spidery legs and transported ashore to museums. Roundout Lighthouse was adopted by the Kingston Maritime Museum, Cape May Lighthouse by the Mid-Atlantic Center for the Arts, Blackwell Island Lighthouse by the New York City Department of Parks & Recreation, and Cove Point Lighthouse by the Calvert Marine Museum, to name only a few. At Tuckerton, New Jersey, and Peconic Bay, Long Island, lost lighthouses were resurrected through the construction of accurate replicas. The sentinels at Fire Island, Sandy Hook, Fort Wadsworth, and Assateague stand preserved on National Park Service lands.

Such heartwarming endings commandeer the pages

Orient Point Lighthouse is the guardian of Oysterponds Reef and a highlight on the ferry crossing from Long Island to Connecticut. Threatened with demolition in 1970, it was saved by public outcry. "This was a place with lots of good stories that local people love to tell," says Merlon E. Wiggin, who wrote a short history of the lighthouse for its centennial celebration in 1999. Among his treasured tales is one of romance and shame. In the 1920s, a keeper of the light fell in love with the daughter of nearby Plum Island Lighthouse. Fetching her for a date meant rowing a considerable distance and dodging ferry traffic. The keeper persevered, won his prize, and the two were married. Unfortunately, he was later discovered supplementing his meager government income by unloading cargo for rumrunners and had to leave town in a hurry.

The Chesapeake Bay's screwpile lighthouses were a distinct architectural style found nowhere else in the nation. "People are surprised to find out not all lighthouses were round stone towers," says the U.S. Lighthouse Society's Chesapeake Chapter president, Anne Puppa. Drum Point Lighthouse is one of only four screwpile sentinels that still stand in the bay.

of modern lighthouse history. Lighthouses today are more apt to be saved than lost, as attitudes about the value of these ancient and often outdated structures have gone from apathetic to impassioned. Interest has grown to the extent that a National Lighthouse Center & Museum now exists on the site of the old lighthouse service depot at Staten Island. Here, in 1852, the newly appointed Lighthouse Board centralized its operations and began an era of progress that made the nation's navigational aids the best in the world by 1900. Now, exhibits grace the 1869 administration building and the 1867 and 1907 lamp shops where lenses and lighting mechanisms were stored and repaired. A restaurant occupies the 1912 machine shop, and the 1864 vaults that once held supplies of oil now support immersion exhibits on lighthouses from around the world.

The Lighthouse Keeper's New Hat

Contrary to popular belief, genuine lighthouse keepers *are* still at work. Their duties have changed, along with their tools and methods, and the job of keeping the lights burning remains important. It simply happens in a new, high-tech way, without need for resident personnel. The Coast Guard Aids to Navigation Teams (ANT) are today's lighthouse keepers. Comprised of specialists in a variety of jobs, the teams visit the automated lights regularly to inspect, repair, and update their many functions. And, contrary to popular belief, they care deeply about these historic structures.

In 1991, the long tradition of lighthouse maintenance brought the crew of the buoy tender *Cowslip* to work at Wolf Trap Lighthouse, a caisson tower built in 1893 on muddy shoals south of where the Rappahannock River pours into the Chesapeake Bay. The men of the *Cowslip* had different concerns as they replaced windows broken by vandals' bullets with durable acrylic panels,

fixed the leaky roof, installed air vents to allow the tower to breathe, and gave the exterior a new coat of bright red paint. A small optic on the cupola had been difficult to service, so the beacon was placed back inside the lantern and its solar panels checked for efficiency. Wolf Trap Light needed a little sprucing, and the crew approached the work compassionately. "This is a strong and sturdy lighthouse," said the *Cowslip*'s chief boatswain's mate. "I really think she'll last another 150 years."

At Brandywine Shoal Light in the Delaware Bay, a Coast Guard crew out of Cape May tended to similar duties in October 2001. The beacon and foghorn, both solar powered, were examined and tested. Bugs and cobwebs disappeared from the lantern; electrical connections were checked and cleaned; burned-out bulbs on the automatic changer were replaced; salt spray was wiped off the windows. "Greenhats" on the team were learning how to do the maintenance under the capable management of Senior Chief Dennis Devers, a former lightkeeper with a deep sense of pride in lighthouse work. The modern optic at Brandywine Shoal Light, he explained to the rookies, works on the same concept as a century-old Fresnel lens. Its intricate inner workings are smaller and more durable, yet still bend and concentrate light like the tower's original prism optic. Caring for the light is "a tradition," according to Devers, "a responsibility that has changed only in practice, not purpose."

It's obvious there's plenty of affection for the old lighthouses amongst ANT crews. The work is not as exciting as search and rescue or drug interdiction, nor as dangerous. It doesn't earn the glamour and respect it had in the old days when keepers resided on the lighthouses. Nonetheless, teams find genuine satisfaction in knowing they keep alive an American institution nearly three centuries old.

The modern counterpart of yesterday's lightkeepers, a Coast Guard Aids to Navigation Team (ANT) out of Cape May, New Jersey, arrives at waterbound Brandywine Shoal Lighthouse for a regular maintenance check. Of particular importance this day is training several "greenhats" who are new to the team. Their work as lighthouse keepers has been altered considerably with modernization, but a solicitous sense of duty to the mariner remains.

THE BOOK THAT SAVED A LIGHTHOUSE

You are still master of the river. Quick, let your light shine again. Each to his own place, little brother!
Hildegard Hoyt Swift, *The Little Red Lighthouse and the Great Gray Bridge*, 1942

Jeffries Hook Light, a tiny beacon marking the eastern shore of the Hudson River in Manhattan, seemed inconsequential when the Coast Guard decided to deactivate and dismantle it in 1947 and auction off the cast-iron parts for scrap metal. The forty-foot tower stood on the tip of Sandy Hook from 1880 to 1917. It was taken apart at the request of the Army, since it stood in the path of gun batteries, and stored at the lighthouse depot on Staten Island. In 1921, the lighthouse was reassembled as a Hudson River beacon in the Washington Heights area and given a bright red daymark. It quickly earned the nickname Lil' Red.

The light's career ended sooner than expected with the construction of the George Washington Bridge in 1931. The great span, with its many lights, dwarfed the small beacon beneath it. The forlorn little tower no longer seemed important, yet it captured the imagination of Hildegard Hoyt Swift, an author and nearby resident. In 1942, she penned *The Little Red Lighthouse and the Great Gray Bridge*, a book for children with the important message that even small things matter. Illustrations by Lynn Ward humanized the diminutive lighthouse, and the book became a popular seller.

Eventually, the Coast Guard decided to extinguish Lil' Red and announced plans to demolish it. What happened next amazed everyone. Children who had read Swift's book began writing letters asking that the lighthouse be spared. Some sent their piggybank coins to save it. The *New York Times* said the tiny lighthouse had become "a symbol of security for many of the city's children" and was "a kind of fairy fortress on the riverbank."

Lil' Red's fate hung in the balance for four years. Then, in July 1951, the city's park commissioner, Robert Moses, was so moved by the children's campaign that he asked the Coast Guard to give the tower to the city. Thus, Lil' Red was spared the wrecking ball, but for nearly twenty years it stood dark, unattended, and rusting. Then, in the 1970s, an elementary student named Matthew Goldin, who had read Swift's book in school, asked his father to help fix up the lighthouse and open it for kids to enjoy. By 1986, the Goldins and their fellow Lil' Red fans had convinced the parks commissioner to restore the tower and make it the centerpiece of Fort Washington Park. Wearing a new red dress and black hat, Lil' Red was given back to the people of New York in a ceremony on May 14, 1991, and received landmark status.

Right and facing page: Individual chapters of the San Francisco–based U.S. Lighthouse Society work within their regions to save historic lighthouses. The granite 1868 Cedar Island Lighthouse is one being rescued by the Long Island Chapter. Bob Muller, president of the group and author of its website, feels strongly about preservation and interpretation of the lighthouse: "It has been the undeserving recipient of vandalism over the years and was gutted by fire in 1974." Defacement shows in the granite plinth over the door, inscribed with the tower's date of establishment.

A bell tower is all that remains of the Fort Washington Lighthouse on the east bank of the Potomac River two miles south of the nation's capital. The lighthouse was little more than a pole beacon on the end of the wharf when approved in 1856 by then–Secretary of War Jefferson Davis. He stipulated that the small sentinel was not to interfere with military operations at the fort and that "the lightkeeper shall be subordinate to the military command of the post." In 1870, the lighthouse tender Tulip constructed a more substantial edifice, though still small by lighthouse standards, and installed a sixth-order lens. The bell tower was added in 1882. In 1901, the lighthouse was demolished and the beacon relocated to the bell tower, which has undergone various updates over the years.

Left: A launch docks at Roundout Lighthouse to drop visitors. The Hudson River Maritime Museum assumed care of the breakwater lighthouse in 1984 in order to preserve an important piece of local history. The first tower here was tended by feminine hands for forty years. Catherine Murdock assumed the job following the death of her husband, who drowned after serving as keeper only a year. Murdock herself nearly drowned in December 1878 when a dam broke at Eddyville, New York, and sent a rush of debris downriver. Her son took over her position upon her retirement in 1907 and served until the current Roundout II lighthouse was built in 1915.

Below: Long Beach Bar Lighthouse in Peconic Bay, Long Island, was reincarnated in 1990 when members of the East End Seaport & Marine Foundation unveiled a replica of the original 1870 structure. It served vessels entering Orient Harbor until 1945, then stood dark and unkempt until 1963 when Independence Day revelers set fire to it. The unique rebuilding project, utilizing blueprints from the National Archives collection, was completed on shore at Greenport Yacht & Shipbuilding in only sixty days, then towed to the site and hoisted onto the old foundation. The lighthouse facsimile serves a dual role as an official Coast Guard beacon and a bed and breakfast.

"New keepers" tend to chores and a baby in a stroller at Maryland's Point Lookout Lighthouse. Automation's legacy has been a mixed blessing—better technology and a reduction in cost for the government, but the loss of day-to-day care at most lighthouses. Volunteers take up the slack to assure that lighthouses still retain a sense of home.

THE CARPENTER GOTHIC LIGHT

This is one of the great success stories of lighthouse preservation.
Steve Murray, Superintendent of Parks, City of North Wildwood

*H*ereford Inlet Lighthouse is the pride of North Wildwood and one of the brightest jewels on the necklace of lights along the Jersey Shore. In a town where tourism could easily eclipse history, citizens have worked hard to preserve this cherished landmark for themselves and future generations. Why? Their lighthouse is unique—a Victorian beauty of "Carpenter Gothic" design, so named for its sturdy stick-style construction and decorative accouterments.

Hereford Inlet Lighthouse went into service in 1874 and was designed by Paul J. Pelz, chief draftsman for the Lighthouse Board. It was built at a time when changing attitudes about utilitarian structures allowed architects to create forms with functional beauty. A gingerbread-style lighthouse would have been a bit too capricious for government tastes, but Hereford Inlet Lighthouse's softly ornate trim and modest colors portrayed a sense of kindness and serenity.

In 1913, storm tides swirled about the base of the lighthouse and began to threaten its foundation. The Bureau of Lighthouses, determined not to lose a vital navigational and treasured public landmark, moved the structure to its present location.

The beacon shone another fifty years, then surrendered its duties to an automatic light on a skeleton tower nearby. Closed up and dark, it was forgotten and grew sadly deteriorated. The city's mayor was anguished by the possibility that one of the oldest buildings in the region might be lost. Citizens pushed to have the lighthouse admitted to both the national and state registers of historic places. In 1982, the city of North Wildwood assumed control of the lighthouse and began formal restoration. As its boarded-up windows were opened and the old paint scraped from its walls, Hereford Inlet Lighthouse received a new lease on life.

Today, as part of a city park, the lighthouse invites visitors to browse its rooms of artifacts and meet the families who lived here for a hundred years. A new optic shines in the lantern, keeping the lighthouse an active navigational aid; the old lens, a glistening chandelier of prisms and brass, stands on display on the first floor. The English garden behind the tower presents a placid, ever-changing vista of light and color. Visitors often find themselves easing into one of the rocking chairs on the lighthouse porch and nodding off, lulled by the soft tumble of waves on the beach and the hum of bees gathering nectar from flowers.

Autumn flowers offer a final burst of color to the gardens at Hereford Inlet Lighthouse. The New Jersey landmark is now a city park and museum.

Take Good Care of the Light

Sighing I climbed the lighthouse stair . . .
And while the day died, sweet and fair,
I lit the lamps again.
Celia Thaxter, "The Wreck of the Pocahontas," 1860

Carole Reily pauses a moment before dinner and gently rings a bell "for our keepers who have crossed the bar." Voices quiet. The names are read, and the bell's soft eulogy carries over the tables where more than twenty former lightkeepers and their families from the Delaware Bay region wait. Eyes are misty, and a few heads bowed. The bell honors individuals, yet rings for a lost era, too. No one will ever again serve in the way these men did or sacrifice as their families have. Lighthouse keepers—standing watch hour by hour, alone on sea-splashed strands, restless sandbars, and hunks of ocean rock—are gone.

But they will never be forgotten, if Carole Reily has her way.

Since 1995, Reily has brought together the Delaware Bay Lighthouse Keepers & Friends Association to keep the flame of memory burning. A diminutive woman, known throughout the region as "The Lighthouse Lady," she has no ties to the service other than a love for light-

houses passed down from her grandfather. His 1905 photograph of Elbow of Cross Ledge Lighthouse, demolished in 1962, captivated Reily and sent her on a mission to save the history of Delaware Bay lighthouses. Along the way, she met a few former Coast Guard lightkeepers and decided to find a way to bring them together and recognize their service. The association is now over two hundred members strong and growing.

Dinner conversation mingles with the clink of silverware against plates and the taps of goblet touching goblet in heartfelt toasts. Gaylord "Dusty" Pierce, vice president of the group and one-time keeper of Fourteen Foot Bank Light, moves from table to table shaking hands and welcoming members. Their backgrounds are diverse. Bill Johnson served on Miah Maull and Ship John Shoal in the 1940s. Carl Ballantine worked on Miah Maull a few years later, and also at Brandywine Shoal. Rod Mulligan was a crewman aboard the lighthouse tender *Zinnia* in the 1960s, serving the Delaware Bay. David Renn worked

Facing page: Shutterbugs from the Delaware Bay Lighthouse Keepers & Friends Association line the rails of a tour boat to photograph Miah Maull Lighthouse in evening light. Many are former lightkeepers with memories of living on the offshore sentinels of the Delaware Bay.

Above: Comfortable in an old Coast Guard Dixie cup and lighthouse t-shirt, Gaylord "Dusty" Pierce makes a pilgrimage to his one-time home on Fourteen Foot Bank Lighthouse. The Delaware Bay caisson-style sentinel was unmanned in 1973, but Pierce recalls livelier days at the lighthouse when a crew of three men shared duties and leisure time. "Those were good times, but tough, too," Pierce admits. "It could get pretty lonely out there." He has experienced a lightkeeper's redux of sorts in recent years as vice president of the Delaware Bay Lighthouse Keepers & Friends Association.

"Everybody loves lighthouses," says Wayne Wheeler, president of the San Francisco–based U.S. Lighthouse Society. A quaint flowerbed centerpiece in North Wildwood, New Jersey (above, left), seems to confirm his assertion. Faux lights are popular lawn ornaments and business logos, especially in areas where a well-known sentinel stands. Assateague Lighthouse's candy-stripe daymark is imitated in a mini golf course decoration in Chincoteague, Virginia (above, right).

on logistics runs to the bay lighthouses and lightships in the late 1960s. William Horn, a retired Coast Guard officer, initiated "Operation Christmas" for the bay lightkeepers in 1970 and oversaw the collection and delivery of gifts to each of the lonely lights.

Reily makes her way to the podium after dessert and calls the meeting to order with the Pledge of Allegiance. She reminds everyone that Fred Ruddick, who served on Ship John Shoal from 1963 to 1964, has brought his detailed model of the lighthouse. The miniature tower is remarkably accurate and will be displayed at several locations, including an elementary school where children can peer through the tiny windows and imagine a tiny lightkeeper at work inside. With luck, they'll learn

something of Ship John Shoal's history. Perhaps children will think of Fred Ruddick living out there on the water long before they were born, keeping a good light so that ships could pass by safely.

Angelo Rigazio stands next to Reily, steadying the podium, helping with the meeting's agenda. He's a member of the board of directors for the Delaware Bay Lighthouse Keepers & Friends Association, a role he considers a personal renaissance of sorts since his departure from Harbor of Refuge Light in 1973 as last officer in charge; he's back in the lighthouse business in a roundabout way. His wife, Darlene, is asked to read the secretary's report to the group, and he smiles warmly as she stands. Even though she was ashore raising the fam-

National Park Service historian Tom Hoffman is among the modern-day lightkeepers who reenact lighthouse service history for a public hungry to experience it. Wearing a replica hat and vest, he stands a memorial watch inside the lantern room at Sandy Hook Light and recollects the days when whale oil and wicks lit the lamps, and ships with billowing white sails passed the hook on their way into busy New York Harbor.

ily when he was on the lighthouse, it was a family duty, Rigazio recalls.

"She kept the light, too, in her own way . . . for me," he explains.

Life has come full circle for the Rigazios and for many others in the room. Their lights have been rekindled in a sense. There's new purpose in keeping the lights now. What is being saved is more than buildings and artifacts, history and memory. Reily's group and others like it are preserving a way of life, the human story of lighthouses.

"They are beautiful, so very beautiful," Reily tells anyone who asks why she devotes so much energy to the cause. "But they are more than bricks and mortar and glass and metal. People built the lighthouses, people

tended them, people made them automatic. And now, only people can save them."

The symbolism endures as well, the intangible reassurance of a light burning in the darkness to guide the hopeful, the weary, the tempest-tossed, even those whose journeys have barely begun.

"Lead, kindly Light, amid the circling gloom. . . . The night is dark, and I am far from home," wrote John Henry Newman almost two hundred years ago. The metaphor in and of itself can't save crumbling masonry or put oil back in the lamps; it can't return the sound of footfall to the stairs or rebuild what has already fallen.

"But it can," Reily says, "inspire a new generation of keepers of the light."

Guide to Mid-Atlantic Lighthouses

This appendix lists existing lighthouses in New York (excluding Lake Ontario and Lake Erie), New Jersey, Delaware, Maryland, and Virginia.

Lights referred to as "active" are currently used as navigational aids and maintained by the U.S. Coast Guard, often in cooperation with museums, historical and preservation societies, or private owners. Some lighthouses maintain commemorative beacons, but these lights no longer serve as guides for ships and do not fall under the care of the Coast Guard.

The list of range lights at the end of the appendix excludes steel skeleton towers and focuses on older, historic range beacons. Not included in the list are faux lights and memorial lights.

A note to lighthouse visitors: Visitors must respect "no trespass" signs placed on lighthouses by the Coast Guard or private owners. Such signs are there for the protection of both the visitors and the often-fragile lighthouses. Many of the lights, especially those offshore, are sealed and locked, and the Coast Guard does not allow anyone to dock on them or climb on them.

The easiest—and probably the most appropriate—way to view lighthouses is from a boat. Ferries and lighthouse cruises abound, and lighthouse lovers should have no trouble getting out onto the water to see their favorites. Please enjoy the mid-Atlantic's lighthouses from the water or other unobtrusive, public vantage points.

New York

Note: While Connecticut claims many lights in Long Island Sound, those included here lie within the geopolitical lines of New York.

Blackwell Island Lighthouse
ROOSEVELT ISLAND

The fifty-foot octagonal gneiss and granite tower was privately built in 1872 and operated by a local family to guide shipping through the perilous East River. The Coast Guard decommissioned it in 1944 during World War II and gave it to the New York City Department of Parks & Recreation. Today it is the focal point of Lighthouse Park on Roosevelt Island.

Cedar Island Lighthouse
SAG HARBOR

A handsome granite tower, this 1868 lighthouse replaced a wooden beacon built in 1839 for the active whaling fleet of Sag Harbor. The island was reconnected to Long Island by fill from the 1938 hurricane. The lighthouse was deactivated in 1934, and a skeleton tower took over its duties.

Coney Island Lighthouse
BROOKLYN

The seventy-foot pile tower was erected in 1890 to guide vessels entering and leaving New York Harbor. A 1,000-pound fogbell was in use until the construction of the Verrazano Narrows Bridge. Automated in 1986, the lighthouse continues to show a flashing red light.

Eatons Neck Lighthouse
HUNTINGTON

Originally fifty feet tall, the 1799 lighthouse was raised to seventy-three feet soon after its construction. The lantern has seen a complete evolution of illuminants, from oil lamps to a third-order lens in 1858 to a modern optic. It stands on an active Coast Guard station.

The rugged walls of the elder sentinel at Cape Henry, Virginia, frame its youthful successor.

Esopus Meadows Lighthouse
ESOPUS

The 1871 light replaced an earlier 1839 tower that was destroyed by a flood. It marks dangerous mudflats called Esopus Meadows. Ice and flooding have ravaged the caisson over the years, and the lighthouse was neglected after automation in 1965. The Save the Esopus Meadows Lighthouse Commission hopes to restore it.

Execution Rocks Lighthouse
NEW ROCHELLE

The forty-two-foot granite tower was built in 1850 to help ships avoid the reef off Sands Point near Hells Gate. Legend holds that the name derives from executions held here in colonial days. The lighthouse was automated and fitted with a modern optic in 1979. Today it is still an active light.

Fire Island Lighthouse
WEST ISLIP

The original octagonal beacon, built in 1826, was replaced by a 168-foot lighthouse in 1858. Cement coating was added in 1871 and a distinctive daymark of black and white bands in 1891. Part of Fire Island National Seashore, it is administered by the Fire Island Lighthouse Preservation Society and is an active lighthouse.

Fort Wadsworth Lighthouse
STATEN ISLAND

Once a beacon for ships passing through "The Narrows," the 1903 tower stands on an old army battery for harbor defense. The light was decommissioned in 1965 after the opening of the Verrazano Narrows Bridge. It is part of the Gateway National Recreational Area.

Great Beds Lighthouse
TOTTENVILLE

Built in 1880 to mark a shoal off Wards Point, the conical cast-iron tower stands sixty feet high. It was automated in 1945 after numerous collisions by passing ships, and its fourth-order lens was replaced with a modern optic.

Horton Point Lighthouse
SOUTHOLD

The square granite tower served Eastern Long Island shipping from 1857 until 1932 when its beacon was transferred to a skeleton tower. Southold Historical Society took over the compound in 1990 and recommissioned the lighthouse as an active aid and museum.

Hudson-Athens Lighthouse
HUDSON CITY

Established in 1874 to guard Middle Ground Flats, the forty-eight-foot lighthouse stands on a stone pier in the Hudson River. It is more than one hundred miles inland and guides ships headed to Albany.

Jeffries Hook Lighthouse
WASHINGTON HEIGHTS

Known to all New Yorkers as "Lil' Red," the tiny cast-iron lighthouse was the Sandy Hook beacon from 1880 to 1917. After transfer to Manhattan in 1921, it served as a channel light for the lower Hudson River. Completion of the George Washington Bridge rendered it obsolete, and it was deactivated in 1947. Today it is the centerpiece in a city park (see chapter 6).

Latimer Reef Lighthouse
FISHERS ISLAND

In 1884, the forty-nine-foot cast-iron caisson lighthouse replaced Eel Grass Lightship, which had anchored near the reef for thirty-five years. The fourth-order lens was automated in 1974, then replaced in 1983 by a solar-powered aero beacon.

Little Gull Island Lighthouse
ORIENT POINT

The original, fifty-five-foot-tall freestone tower, built in 1805, proved inadequate to guide vessels past Great Gull Island. It was replaced in 1869 by a granite lighthouse, eighty-one feet tall, on a stone pier. The 1938 hurricane damaged the station, and a fire in 1944 destroyed the keeper's house. The light was automated in 1978 and is still active today.

Lloyd Harbor Lighthouse
HUNTINGTON

The first tower, built in 1857, was brick and attached to a wood-frame keeper's house. Discontinued in 1924, a fire destroyed it twenty-four years later. In the meantime, a second lighthouse was built on the harbor—the first reinforced concrete lighthouse on the mainland East Coast. This 1912 lighthouse was called Huntington Harbor Lighthouse until the decommissioning of the original tower. Thereafter it was called Lloyd Harbor Lighthouse, though some people still call it by its former name.

Sturdy granite walls hold up the iron housetop lantern of Old Field Point Lighthouse in Long Island Sound.

Long Beach Bar Lighthouse

ORIENT HARBOR

This lighthouse was established in 1870 and originally called "Bug Light" for the pile legs on which it stood. The cottage-style beacon was given a concrete foundation in 1924. Following deactivation in 1945, the structure was destroyed by fire. Rebuilt by the East End Seaport & Marine Foundation, the tower was relit in 1990 as an official Coast Guard beacon, and the lighthouse is operated as a bed and breakfast.

Montauk Point Lighthouse

MONTAUK

New York's oldest lighthouse, established in 1797, the 110-foot octagonal tower was one of twelve lights ordered by George Washington during his first term of office. Automated in 1987, it is still an active light. Both the tower and keeper's house are a museum operated by the Montauk Historical Society.

North Dumpling Lighthouse

FISHERS ISLAND

Situated on an island in eastern Long Island Sound, the site was purchased from the Pequots in 1640 and sold to the federal government in 1847. The original 1848 wooden lighthouse was replaced in 1871 with a French Second Empire structure. The light was deactivated in 1959. Private owners have altered the site considerably, but the Coast Guard reactivated the beacon in 1989 and still maintains it. The lighthouse is not open to the public.

Old Field Point Lighthouse

OLD FIELD

To warn ships of a crooked finger of land east of Smithtown Bay, a thirty-foot plastered stone lighthouse was placed at Old Field Point in 1824. Its original, detached, stone keeper's house remains, but the tower was updated in 1868. A skeleton tower took over its duties in 1933.

Old Orchard Lighthouse
OAKWOOD BEACH

When first lighted in 1893, the tower acted as a front range beacon in partnership with the Waackaack Light to guide vessels through the Gedney Channel. The rear range was discontinued in 1939, and Old Orchard became a channel lighthouse. It was automated in 1955.

Orient Point Lighthouse
ORIENT POINT

The forty-five-foot caisson light, established in 1899, marks Oyster Pond Reef and Plum Gut in Long Island Sound. Automated in 1954, it was threatened with demolition in 1970 due to a five-degree tilt. Public outcry won it a reprieve, and it continues to operate.

Plum Island Lighthouse
ORIENT

The first tower, a thirty-foot stone edifice built in 1827, had structural faults and was replaced in 1869 with a Gothic Revival lighthouse. Automated in 1968, the sentinel shares its island with the U.S. Department of Agriculture's Plum Island Animal Disease Center. It was deactivated in 1978.

Princes Bay Lighthouse
STATEN ISLAND

Overlooking an important bay on the shipping route to New York Harbor, the original 1828 lighthouse was wood. Replaced by a brownstone tower in 1864, during the Civil War, the beacon had an unusual three-and-a-half-order Fresnel lens. In 1922, a steel skeleton tower upstaged the lighthouse, which was sold to a nearby Catholic mission that placed a religious statue on the empty lantern deck. The lighthouse is currently closed to the public, but the New York State Trust for Public Land recently acquired the property and plans to restore the tower for public use.

Race Rock Lighthouse
FISHERS ISLAND

Considered a monumental engineering feat, the forty-five-foot lighthouse of Gothic Revival style was built in 1879 and sits on an artificial island submerged in the bottleneck of western Long Island Sound. Automated in 1978, its beacon flashes alternating red and white.

Robbins Reef Lighthouse
STATEN ISLAND

Established in 1839 to guard the Seal Rocks, the fifty-six-foot caisson tower replaced a white stone tower in 1883 and guides ships into Upper New York Bay. Its original fourth-order lens was replaced by a modern optic during automation in 1966.

Romer Shoal Lighthouse
NEW YORK

Originally a test tower at the Staten Island Lighthouse Depot, the cast-iron tower was moved to Romer Shoal in the Swash Channel and reassembled on a caisson foundation in 1898. Automated in 1966, it shows a red beacon toward land and a white beacon toward water.

Roundout Lighthouse
KINGSTON

The station was established in 1837, but spring flooding of Roundout Creek destroyed the site's first two lighthouses. A brick sentinel built on a sturdy stone caisson in 1915 has fared better. Now in the care of the Hudson River Maritime Museum, it is an active Coast Guard lighthouse and open for public tours.

Sands Point Lighthouse
NORTH HEMPSTEAD

Established in 1809, the eighty-foot freestone tower guided ships on the final approach to New York Harbor through Hells Gate, a bottleneck between Long Island and Connecticut. The original tower was replaced by a skeleton tower in 1922. Privately owned since 1924 and declared a New York State Landmark in 1994, it has had many illustrious occupants, including William Randolph Hearst. It is not open to the public.

Saugerties Lighthouse
SAUGERTIES

Built to mark the entrance to Esopus Creek, the current 1869 lighthouse replaced an 1836 structure destroyed by a flood. The lighthouse was abandoned and deactivated in 1954 and stood empty for many years. The Saugerties Lighthouse Conservancy now operates it as a bed and breakfast.

Stepping Stones Lighthouse
KINGS POINT

Built in 1877, the beautiful thirty-eight-foot Second Empire sentinel warns of reefs east of Throgs Neck. The light was automated in 1966, when its classical fifth-order lens was replaced with a modern optic. It is still an active light.

Stony Point Lighthouse
HENDERSON
The oldest lighthouse on the Hudson River, the diminutive sentinel was established in 1826 and marks the entrance to the Hudson Highlands. Its elevation has protected it from ice and floods for nearly three centuries. It was deactivated in 1925. Now part of the Stony Point Battlefield State Historic Site, its beacon was relighted in 1995.

Stratford Shoal Lighthouse
PORT JEFFERSON
Also known as Middle Ground Light, the 1877 Gothic Revival tower replaced a lightship anchored here for forty years. The sentinel was automated in 1970 and converted to solar power in the 1980s.

Tarrytown Lighthouse
TARRYTOWN
Established in 1883, the quaint caisson sentinel was originally positioned a quarter mile offshore in the Hudson River. It was moved to the east shore a short distance north of the Tappan Zee Bridge after it was decommissioned in 1961. It now serves as a public landmark in Westchester County.

New Jersey

Ambrose Light Tower
ROCKAWAY POINT
The Texas tower–style lighthouse stands in ninety feet of water, seven miles at sea on the site of the old Ambrose Lightship—the primary sentry for New York Bay. Built in 1967, it is the newest mid-Atlantic lighthouse. The original tower was manned until 1988. It was rebuilt in 1999 after being hit by a tanker in 1996 (see chapter 4).

Absecon Lighthouse
ATLANTIC CITY
The 171-foot tower was built over "Graveyard Inlet" in 1857 and stood a lonely watch before the rise of Atlantic City. Deactivated in 1933, it was given to the state thirty years later and has been restored, relighted, and opened to the public.

Barnegat Inlet Lighthouse
BARNEGAT
The first tower on this location, built in 1835, was too short and was replaced in 1859 by a 175-foot lighthouse

A dark center band distinguishes Atlantic City's Absecon Lighthouse from its nearby compatriots. It is one of three tall coastal lighthouses guarding southern New Jersey.

to guard Barnegat Inlet. It was downgraded in importance in 1927 with the anchoring of a lightship off Long Beach and was extinguished in 1944. It is now the focal point of Barnegat State Park.

Brandywine Shoal Lighthouse
CAPE MAY
A lightship served on the site from 1823 until 1850. Attempts were made to build a pile lighthouse, but ice destroyed it. A screwpile structure, completed in 1850, proved solid and stood until 1914 when a new concrete caisson lighthouse went into service. Keepers remained on the light until its automation in 1974.

Cape May Lighthouse
CAPE MAY
Established in 1824, this was the first lighthouse to mark

Towering 175 feet over Long Beach Island, Barnegat Inlet Light exemplifies the tall seacoast sentinel.

Cape May Lighthouse's red lantern stands out well against the blue skies of southern New Jersey.

the north side of the Delaware Bay. The original sixty-eight-foot brick tower was of poor quality, and a more substantial tower replaced it in 1847. A decade later, the present 157-foot lighthouse was built to accommodate a first-order lens. The station remains active and is a museum operated by the Mid-Atlantic Center for the Arts.

East Point Lighthouse
HEISLERVILLE
Originally called Maurice River Lighthouse, the 1849 cottage-style sentinel served traffic on the east shore of the Delaware Bay. The lighthouse was abandoned in 1941 and burned in 1971. The Maurice River Historical Society has restored it, relighting it with a commemorative beacon in 1980.

Fourteen Foot Bank Lighthouse
BOWERS BEACH
Marking Joe Flogger Shoal west of the main shipping

channel in the Delaware Bay, the 1887 cast-iron lighthouse replaced a lightship anchored on the site since 1876. It was the first sentinel built on a caisson sunk by the pneumatic process. Automated in 1973, it now operates as a solarized light.

Hereford Inlet Lighthouse
NORTH WILDWOOD
The wooden stick-style lighthouse, rising fifty feet, was built in 1874 to aid the fishing fleet of the old village of Anglesea. Moved back from the ocean's edge in 1914, it served another fifty years before being deactivated. After four years of restoration, the lighthouse was opened as a museum and relighted in 1986 (see chapter 6).

Miah Maull Lighthouse
FORTESCUE
Established in 1909, this is the youngest lighthouse site on the Delaware Bay. It is named for a hazardous shoal

just east of the main shipping channel on which pilot Nehemiah Maull was shipwrecked. The light has operated automatically since 1973.

Navesink Twin Lights
HIGHLANDS

The only twin lights in the Mid-Atlantic, the rugged stone towers were built in 1828 and rebuilt in 1862. They served as landfall lights for the port of New York. Following deactivation in 1952, the station became Twin Lights State Historic Site, and the towers were ceremoniously relighted in 1962.

Sandy Hook Lighthouse
HIGHLANDS

The oldest standing lighthouse in the nation, the eighty-eight-foot octagonal tower has seen almost continuous service since 1764 as a beacon for vessels headed into New York Bay. It was automated in 1965. It is still an active light and is part of Gateway National Recreational Area.

Sea Girt Lighthouse
SEA GIRT

Built in 1896, the Victorian-style brick house rises fifty-two feet. It served as a beacon for Sea Girt Inlet. Retired in 1945, it was restored and relighted in 1983 by the Sea Girt Lighthouse Citizens Committee.

Delaware

Delaware Breakwater East Lighthouse
LEWES

Built in 1885 to replace the defunct Cape Henlopen beacon, the forty-nine-foot cast-iron lighthouse perches on the east end of the Delaware Breakwater. In 1903, it was changed to a front range light for a period of fifteen years, then resumed its role as a breakwater light until it was abandoned after World War II. The light was deactivated in 1996.

Fenwick Island Lighthouse
OCEAN CITY

Built in 1859, this is the oldest existing lighthouse in Delaware. The eighty-seven-foot brick tower stands near the transpeninsular marker used by surveyors to estab-

Fenwick Island Lighthouse rises above surrounding homes at Ocean City, Delaware.

lish the famous Mason-Dixon Line and guided vessels approaching from the south to the Delaware Bay. The light was deactivated in 1978. Friends of Fenwick Island Lighthouse relighted the tower in 1982 and currently maintain it.

Harbor of Refuge Lighthouse
LEWES

Marking the southern end of the National Harbor of Refuge, the first tower was a wooden structure atop a caisson, built in 1902. It was destroyed in a storm, and the current light was built in 1926 on the original caisson. The light was automated in 1973.

Mispillion Lighthouse
SLAUGHTER BEACH

Three lighthouses stood at the mouth of the Mispillion River between the site's establishment in 1831 and 1873 when the current wooden frame tower was built. Converted to automatic operation with acetylene gas in 1911, the lighthouse was discontinued and sold. The beacon moved to a skeleton tower in 1929.

Ship John Shoal Lighthouse
GREENWICH

Construction begun in 1854 resulted in a foundation, but the lighthouse was not completed and lit until 1874. Made of cast iron, the entire structure is painted red and includes an attached concrete platform. The light was automated in 1973 and is still active.

Maryland

Baltimore Lighthouse
BALTIMORE

Among the Chesapeake Bay's youngest sentinels, this 1908 light marks a shoal in the Baltimore Channel near the mouth of the Magothy River. The caisson foundation supports a brick dwelling. Automated since 1964, it was sealed in 1983 to prevent vandalism. The flashing white beacon still guides shipping as approaching Baltimore from the south.

Bloody Point Bar Lighthouse
KENT ISLAND

The fifty-four-foot caisson light was built in 1882 to mark a sandbar near the deepest part of the Chesapeake Bay shipping channel at the entrance to the Eastern Bay. Gutted by fire in 1960, it was closed up and automated. Today it is still an active beacon.

Concord Point Lighthouse
HAVRE DE GRACE

The original 1827 stone tower stands watch at the mouth of the Susquehanna River. Automated in 1920, it was adopted by the Friends of Concord Point Lighthouse after deactivation in 1975. A museum operates in the old keeper's house.

Cove Point Lighthouse
LUSBY

The fifty-one-foot stone tower was built in 1828 to guide vessels into the Patuxent River. Automated in 1986, the lighthouse is still active and is maintained by the Calvert Marine Museum.

Drum Point Lighthouse
SOLOMONS

Built in 1883 to warn of a shoal at the entrance to the Patuxent River, the little beacon was automated in 1960 and closed two years later. It was moved to Calvert Marine Museum in 1975, restored to its 1880s heyday, and now serves as an exhibit.

Fishing Battery Lighthouse
ABERDEEN

A cottage-style sentinel with a black lantern, this 1853 beacon sits on Blackwater National Wildlife Refuge. Abandoned in 1921, it was upstaged by a skeleton tower beacon and has deteriorated.

Fort Washington Lighthouse
TANTALLON

Built in 1857 to mark the Potomac River channel where it joins the Piscataway Creek, the diminutive sentinel was rebuilt in 1882, then moved to the station bell tower in 1901. Its red beacon still shines from the wharf of old Fort Washington.

Hooper Island Lighthouse
HOOPERSVILLE

One of Chesapeake Bay's youngest sentinels, the sixty-three-foot caisson tower has warned of shoals between Smith Point and Cove Point since 1902. It was automated in 1961. Vandals stole the priceless prism lens in 1976, and it was replaced by a solar-powered optic.

Hooper Strait Lighthouse
ST. MICHAELS

A lightship marked the channel through Hooper Strait in 1827. The first screwpile lighthouse on the site, built in 1867, was destroyed by ice, and a second screwpile lighthouse was built in 1879. After it was abandoned in 1954, the lighthouse was moved from Tangier Sound to the grounds of the Chesapeake Bay Maritime Museum.

Piney Point Lighthouse
VALLEY LEE

The squat thirty-five-foot stone tower stands fourteen miles inside the entrance to the Potomac River. From 1836 to 1964, it warned of shoals off the point. Automated in 1939, it was transferred to the St. Clement's Island Potomac River Museum.

Point Lookout Lighthouse
SCOTLAND

Built in 1830 to mark the entrance to the Potomac River, the first beacon sat atop a small house. In 1883, a second floor was added to elevate the light. It continued to serve until 1965 when the beacon was moved to a steel tower and the lighthouse was turned over to the U.S. Navy. The Maryland Department of Natural Resources maintains the exterior as part of a state park and opens the tower for tours.

Hooper Island Lighthouse shines in the distance off Tilghman Island in the Chesapeake Bay.

Point No Point Lighthouse
DAMERON

Established in 1905, the fifty-two-foot caisson lighthouse fills a dark space along Chesapeake Bay's main shipping channel between Cove Point and Point Lookout. Although the light was automated in 1938, Coast Guard personnel continued to reside in the tower until 1962.

Pooles Island Lighthouse
ABERDEEN

The rugged stone tower stands on an island just south of the Susquehanna River's egress. It was built in 1825, automated in 1917 after the compound became U.S. Army property, and discontinued in 1939 when the island was given to the War Department. Today it is surrounded by Aberdeen Proving Ground.

Seven Foot Knoll Lighthouse
BALTIMORE

The oldest existing screwpile lighthouse on the Chesapeake Bay, this all-iron sentinel was constructed in 1855 to mark a dangerous shoal in the Patapsco River. Automated in 1948, the beacon continued to shine until the 1980s when it was replaced by a skeleton tower. The lighthouse was dismantled and moved to Baltimore's Inner Harbor to serve as a museum, owned by the Baltimore Maritime Museum.

Sandy Point Shoal Lighthouse
ANNAPOLIS

This light was originally built as a cottage-style lighthouse on Sandy Point in 1858. The lighthouse was replaced with an offshore caisson tower in 1883 to better mark the shoals where ships make an important turn on the way to Baltimore. Unmanned in 1963, the tower continues in operation with a flashing white beacon.

Sharps Island Lighthouse
TILGHMAN ISLAND

Three towers have stood at Sharps Island. The first, built in 1837, was a simple housetop affair. Erosion forced the construction of a screwpile lighthouse in 1865, which was carried away by ice in 1881. The current caisson tower was lit a year later, shortly before the island disappeared. Ice and erosion have caused the tower to lean, but the light is still active.

Solomons Lump Lighthouse
CRISFIELD

The original 1875 screwpile tower, marking Kedge's

Relentless ice jams in the Chesapeake Bay have pushed Sharps Island Lighthouse decidedly out of plumb.

Strait Shoals, was destroyed by ice in 1893. A caisson tower replaced it in 1895. Automated in 1950, the dwelling was removed, leaving only a square light tower, which still serves as an active light.

Thomas Point Shoal Lighthouse
ANNAPOLIS

In 1875, the lighthouse replaced an 1825 masonry tower established to mark a dangerous shoal at the entrance to the South River. It is the only active screwpile tower in the bay on its original site. It was automated in 1986.

Turkey Point Lighthouse
ELK NECK

The thirty-eight-foot white stone tower, built in 1833, overlooks the head of the Chesapeake Bay where the Northeast and Susquehanna Rivers arrive. Automated in 1947, it is part of Elk Neck State Park.

Virginia

Assateague Lighthouse

CHINCOTEAGUE

The original 1833 tower was replaced in 1867 by a 142-foot brick lighthouse with a first-order Fresnel lens. Known for its distinctive red and white daymark, the sentinel was automated in 1965 and stands on Chincoteague National Wildlife Refuge.

Cape Charles Lighthouse

KIPTOPEKE

A sixty-foot masonry tower stood on Smith Island at the northern entrance to Chesapeake Bay from 1828 until 1864 when a brick tower replaced it. The present 184-foot pile lighthouse was built in 1895, automated in 1963, and shows a white light for twenty-four miles.

Cape Henry Lighthouse, New

VIRGINIA BEACH

The 157-foot cast-iron tower was built in 1882 to replace the elder Cape Henry Light (see following listing). Unmanned in 1984, it shows a white light for seventeen miles to help ships entering Chesapeake Bay and a red sector to mark dangerous shoals.

Cape Henry Lighthouse, Old

VIRGINIA BEACH

The oldest lighthouse on Chesapeake Bay, the octagonal stone tower marked the bay's entrance from 1791 until a newer light was built nearby in 1882. Adopted by the Association for the Preservation of Virginia Antiquities in 1930, it is now a public landmark at Fort Story.

Chesapeake Light

VIRGINIA BEACH

A lightship served as a welcome beacon for the Chesapeake Bay from 1933 until 1965 when the ultra-modern Texas tower was built. The youngest lighthouse on the bay, it stands in 117 feet of water fourteen miles off Cape Henry. It was automated in 1980 (see chapter 4).

Jones Point Lighthouse

ALEXANDRIA

The small clapboard sentinel, built in 1856, warned vessels of sandbars in the Potomac River just south of Washington, D.C. Replaced by a skeleton tower in 1926, its beacon continued to shine until 1962. Although owned by the National Park Service, the lighthouse is cared for by the Mount Vernon chapter of the Daughters of the American Revolution, who relighted it in the late 1990s.

New Point Comfort Lighthouse

BAVON

Showing the way to Mobjack Bay and the York River, the 1804 octagonal brick tower served until erosion threatened it. The fifty-eight-foot lighthouse was abandoned in 1963, and vandalism and weather have taken a toll on it in recent years.

Newport News Middle Ground Lighthouse

NEWPORT NEWS

Warning of Middle Ground Shoal in Hampton Roads, the fifty-two-foot caisson tower went into service in 1891 with a fourth-order Fresnel lens. Automated in 1954, it was converted to solar power with a modern optic in 1988.

Old Point Comfort Lighthouse

HAMPTON

The second-oldest lighthouse on Chesapeake Bay, the fifty-four-foot octagonal stone tower was established in 1802 and marks the entrance to Hampton Roads. Though automated in 1972 and still active, it retains its fourth-order Fresnel lens.

Smith Point Lighthouse

REEDVILLE

Five lighthouses and one lightship have marked the point along the southern approach to the Potomac River since 1802. The current fifty-two-foot caisson lighthouse was built in 1897 and automated in the 1970s.

Thimble Shoal Lighthouse

HAMPTON

The original tower was a screwpile structure built in 1872 to warn of shoals near the Hampton Roads channel. It burned in 1909 and was rebuilt as a fifty-five-foot iron caisson tower in 1914. The tower was automated in 1964.

Wolf Trap Lighthouse

MATHEWS

First guarded by a lightship, shoals at the entrance to the Rappahannock River were marked by a fifty-two-foot caisson lighthouse in 1894. Automated in 1971, the lighthouse shows a flashing white light.

Bright red stripes identify Assateague Lighthouse amidst its verdant surroundings in a national wildlife refuge at Chincoteague, Virginia.

Range Lights

Bellevue Rear Range Light
EDGEMOOR, DELAWARE

The 104-foot pyramidal iron tower overlooks the Christiana River near the marine terminal at Wilmington. When built in 1909, it worked with a wooden front range that was positioned on the shores of the Delaware River, but when the channel was dredged, that front range needed to be moved to the shores of the Christiana River. A new steel front range tower was built in 1929, and the two beacons continued in service until the rear range light was replaced by a steel tower in 2000.

Chapel Hill Light and Conover Beacon
LEONARDO, NEW JERSEY

The structures at Chapel Hill and Conover were established in 1856 and once worked together as the Chapel Hill Range Lights, helping vessels move in and out of the Navesink River. The discontinued Chapel Hill Light is now privately owned. It was replaced by an automated skeleton tower in 1940 that teams with the Conover Beacon to provide a range for Chapel Hill Channel.

Craighill Channel Lower Range Lights
HART ISLAND, BALTIMORE, MARYLAND

Leading from the Chesapeake Bay into the Patapsco River and Baltimore Harbor, Craighill Channel was named in honor of Lighthouse Board member William Price Craighill upon its completion in 1870. The lower range lights that marked the channel consisted of two sentinels situated about two and a half miles apart. The front light was a cast-iron caisson structure thirty-nine feet tall, and the rear beacon perched 105 feet atop an iron frame pyramidal tower enclosing a square Victorian house. The rear range house was demolished years ago, but both towers and beacons remain functional.

Craighill Channel Upper Range Lights
SPARROW POINT, BALTIMORE, MARYLAND

Cutoff Channel, opened in the early 1880s, provides a link between the Craighill and Brewerton channels leading into Baltimore Harbor. Upper range lights for the channel were built in 1886 and consist of a short octagonal brick front tower—the first caisson lighthouse built in the United States—and an iron frame rear tower. The front tower is well known for its bright red and white banded daymark.

Finns Point Rear Range Light
PENNS NECK, NEW JERSEY

Established in 1877, the ninety-four-foot wrought-iron tower once worked in tandem with a front range to provide guidance through a difficult turn in the Delaware River. Widening of the channel necessitated a new alignment and made the range at Finns Point obsolete. It was deactivated in 1950. Refurbished by a local preservation group, the rear range tower is open to the public on special occasions. The front range beacon was demolished.

Liston Front and Rear Range Lights
PORT PENN, DELAWARE

Standing at the entrance to the Delaware River, these were the first ranges encountered on the route to Philadelphia. The front range was established in 1904 and originally shone from the top of a shoreline house, now privately owned, before being moved to a skeleton tower in 1953. A tall iron rear range light is almost three miles inland, making this the longest range in the United States, visible from twenty miles.

Marcus Hook Rear Range Light
CLAYMONT, DELAWARE

Located on the western banks of the Delaware River, this range guides ships past perils along the Pennsylvania-Delaware border. The front range light, built in 1918, was the first automated acetylene gas light on the river. The rear range came into service in 1920 in a 105-foot reinforced concrete tower and was automated in the 1950s. Both lights continue in service.

The pile-design Cape Charles Lighthouse has stood watch over Smith Island on the northern entrance to the Chesapeake Bay since 1895.

New Dorp Light and Elm Tree Light
STATEN ISLAND, NEW YORK

Established in 1856 and marking the Swash channel, the range consisted of a forty-foot cottage-style sentinel at New Dorp and a sixty-foot hexagonal wooden tower at Elm Tree. In 1899, the Elm Tree tower was moved due to changes in the channel. It was replaced by a concrete tower in 1939 and deactivated in 1964. The New Dorp Lighthouse is privately owned. Elm Tree Light stands on an old airfield in Gateway National Recreational Area.

Reedy Island Rear Range Light
ODESSA, DELAWARE

Situated on the Delaware River between Appoquinimink and Blackbird Creeks, the station began with simple post beacons in 1904. By 1906 a cottage-style front light was completed, followed in 1910 by a 125-foot iron tower to serve as the rear light. A steel tower replaced the front range in 1951, but the 1910 rear range tower remains in service.

Staten Island Light and West Bank Light
AMBROSE CHANNEL, NEW YORK

Cast-iron West Bank Light, built in 1901, operated as a single beacon until 1912 when the ornate brick tower at Staten Island was constructed and made a partner in the range marking the center of the Ambrose Channel. Staten Island Light was designated a New York City Landmark in 1968.

Tinicum Rear Range Light
PAULSBORO, NEW JERSEY

Established in 1880, the wrought-iron tower rises 110 feet above water. It partners with a shorter front range beacon to mark a dangerous turn and bar in the Delaware River. While the front range was moved to a steel tower in 1908, the rear range continues to serve in the original lighthouse, which is now in the care of the Tinicum Rear Range Lighthouse Society (see chapter 4).

The iron-frame Craighill Channel Rear Lower Range Light works with three other beacons to ensure safe passage into Baltimore Harbor.

Bibliography

———◦———

Bachand, Robert G. *Northeast Lights.* Norwalk, Conn.: Sea Sports Publications, 1989.

Bailey, John. *Sentinel of the Jersey Cape.* Cape May, N.J.: Mid-Atlantic Center for the Arts, 1989.

Beach, John W. *Cape Henlopen Lighthouse and Delaware Breakwater.* Dover, Del.: Dover Litho Printing Co., 1970.

Clifford, Candace. *Inventory of Historic Light Stations.* Washington, D.C.: National Park Service, 1994.

Clifford, Mary Louise, and J. Candace Clifford. *Women Who Kept the Lights.* Williamsburg, Va.: Cypress Communications, 1993.

Crowley, Jim. *Lighthouses of New York.* Saugerties, N.Y.: Hope Farm Press, 2000.

deGast, Robert. *The Lighthouses of the Chesapeake.* Baltimore, Md.: Johns Hopkins University, 1973.

DeWire, Elinor. *Guardians of the Lights: Stories of Lighthouse Keepers.* Sarasota, Fla.: Pineapple Press, 1995.

Gately, Bill. *Sentinels of the Shore: A Guide to the Lighthouses and Lightships of New Jersey.* Harvey Cedars, N.J.: Down the Shore Publishing, 1998.

Glunt, Ruth. *Lights and Legends of the Hudson.* Monroe, N.Y.: Library Research Associates, 1975.

Gowdy, Jim, and Kim Ruth. *Guiding Lights of the Delaware River & Bay.* Egg Harbor City, N.J.: Laureate Press, 1999.

Grant, John, and Ray Jones. *Legendary Lighthouses.* Old Saybrook, Conn.: Globe Pequot Press, 1998.

Hamilton, Harlan. *Lights & Legends: A Historical Guide to Lighthouses of Long Island Sound, Fishers Island Sound, and Block Island Sound.* Stamford, Conn.: Wescott Cove Publishing, 1987.

Harrison, Tim, and Ray Jones. *Endangered Lighthouses.* Guilford, Conn.: Globe Pequot Press, 2001.

Harrison, Tim, and Ray Jones. *Lost Lighthouses.* Guilford, Conn.: Globe Pequot Press, 2000.

Holland, F. Ross. *Great American Lighthouses.* Washington, D.C.: Preservation Press, 1989.

Houghton, George. *Sandy Hook in 1879.* Golden, Colo.: Outbooks, 1981.

Jones, Stephen. *Harbor of Refuge.* New York: W.W. Norton, 1981.

Kochel, Kenneth. Revised & Updated by Jeremy D'Entremont. *Atlantic Coast Lighthouses.* Wells, Maine: Lighthouse Digest, 2000.

Noble, Dennis L. *Lighthouses and Keepers: The U.S. Lighthouse Service and its Legacy.* Annapolis, Md.: Naval Institute Press, 1997.

Putnam, George R. *Sentinel of the Coasts.* New York: Norton, 1937.

Roberts, Bruce, and Ray Jones. *Mid-Atlantic Lighthouses: Hudson River to Chesapeake Bay.* Old Saybrook, Conn.: Globe Pequot Press, 1996

Turbyville, Linda. *Bay Beacons: Lighthouses of the Chesapeake Bay.* Annapolis, Md.: Eastwind Publishing, 1995.

Index

About the Author and Photographer

Photograph by Jonathan DeWire

Photograph by Abe Kreworuka

Elinor DeWire

Elinor DeWire has been researching lighthouses for more than twenty-five years. She has written six books and more than fifty articles on the topic. Her travels to more than four hundred lighthouses worldwide are the focus of her lectures and articles. Audiences from Maine to Hawaii have enjoyed her slide presentations on lighthouses, and she has discussed the topic on various radio and television programs throughout the United States. She writes columns for *The Beachcomber* and *Lighthouse Digest*. She also serves in a variety of capacities for several non-profit lighthouse preservation groups and chairs the youth initiative for the American Lighthouse Foundation.

Paul Eric Johnson

Paul Eric Johnson is the Director of Photography for the Wohlfarth Galleries in Washington D.C. and Provincetown, Cape Cod. His recent work includes "Re-imagine New England," a portfolio of laser-exposed fine photographic prints. He teaches at the Cape Cod Photo Workshops and is the resident photographer for electronicgrange.net, a cyber-cafe in Weld, Maine. His photography is published throughout the world in books, magazines, calendars, and advertising, for such organizations as Time-Life, the Sierra Club, *Saveur*, *Travel & Leisure*, *Historic Preservation*, the *Boston Globe*, NBC, Polaroid, Calvin Klein, and Castle Rock Entertainment.